MAGICAL CROWS, RAVENS AND THE CELEBRATION OF DEATH

By Andrew Steed

COPYRIGHT

DEDICATION

This book is dedicated to Joyce Helen Sivers. Joyce reminds me of the Morrighan — she is regal, strong, elegant, wise and she speaks her truth powerfully in the world. I gladly gave my heart to her the day we met. I know that I have walked beside this Dragon Queen in a previous lifetime. I have swum with her too in the land of the Merfolk! In this lifetime Joyce stands by my side, shoulder-to-shoulder and back-to-back. She is my rock, my love and best friend — Thank you for all of your support and guidance Joyce — I love you!

ACKNOWLEDGEMENTS

A huge thank you to the Morrighan, the crows and ravens who have shaped my life and who are the true stars of this story. Thank you to the ancestors, the 'Celtic' Saints and monks who recorded the stories of the Dagda's Harp, of the Tuatha Dé Danann and the Mabinogion. Thank you to the bards of old who wove stories through the ages that are as relevant to our lives today as when they were first told.

Thank you Joyce for your love, trust and for sharing this wild ride with me. Thank you to all of the pilgrims who have trusted me to guide them on magical adventures. My children Christy and Aylish and my grandaughter Muirín for choosing to walk this magical pathway with me.

Thanks to Davy Patton and Cathy O'Neill, the guardians of the Morrighan's Cave, who shared the way to the cave, opened their home to me and welcomed me to sit by their hearth.

Thanks to Ambu, Feroz Jiju and Anudaj for paving the way for me to dance in the magic of the Crow Festival.

Thank you Marilyn Derstine for the hours, dedication and talent in the editing process. You have made this an even better book because of your love, gifts and diligence.

Thank you Mike and Jenn Fenster, your support and friendship means the world to both Joyce and I.

Thanks to Nicole Pisaniello for producing such a beautiful painting for the front cover and to Steph Brown for bringing the magic of the text and border to complete a phenomenal front and back cover.

Thanks to my parents Anthony John Robert Steed and Elizabeth Grace Steed, Andrea Linebaugh, Jan and Mike Gale, Natalya Elliott, Doron Alon, David Reid, Margaret Greer, Pat Beck, Christy Davidson, Ryan Flannery, Whispy, to the Mitchell Clan, all of the Fife ancestors, Bonnie, Snuggles, the Weegie and Fifer beings who bring us such joy and to all of the unnamed beings who have helped shape me in this life journey. Séa.

Magic.

What does it mean to you?

For some it is a world of fantasy. A world of unicorns and rainbows and daydreams. But true magic is more than empty wishful longings to simply make things so. Armchair detectives and the like never changed any outcomes. For if you wish to make a difference, it is as Shakespeare wrote so long ago, "Once more unto the breach, dear friends, once more…The game's afoot. Follow your spirit…."

You must engage with tripartite action of body, mind, and spirit.

But while there are those that sit in idle reverie, there are also those who refuse to entertain the possibility of magic at all. They say it is but a tool of deception, wielded by charlatans and deceivers for personal profit.

Still others say it does not exist at all in any form. But let us take pause and look deeply into reality. Let us look into the betwixt and between of our everyday perceptions. Let us peer into the constructs that bind us. If we put aside the math, quantum physics (the loop gravity version, at least) tells us three important things.

- The Universe is finite and granular. In other words, although they are very tiny, there is a limit to the minuteness of the particles that make up ourselves and the world we live in. The Universe has limits.

- The Universe is random. Although we desire order, rules, and regularity, a degree of chaos is a fundamental characteristic of our existence. Chance is a vital element in our existence.

- The Universe is relational. We do not exist in a Universe of isolated, observable things. Things are defined by, they only exist by, understanding them in relationship to one another. The very blueprint of the Universe requires an interconnectedness of all things.

Let us focus on the implications of that last bit, for it truly transforms our perspective. It means that electrons are far from the little moons of negative charge that orbit about a positively charged nucleus as many of us were taught not so long ago. It implies, for example, that electrons are defined only by their interactions with other particles. Yet, here is the most astonishing fact. In between these interactions that define their being, electrons quite literally cease to exist. In other words, electrons blink in and out of reality like Christmas tree lights.

Just about every living multicellular organism on this planet contains mitochondria. These cellular organelles are the power supplies that provide the chemical energy that sustains life. It does this by utilizing a reaction called the Krebs cycle. Bacteria utilize this same chemical process, also known as the citric acid cycle, by performing it within their cytoplasm.

This reaction is the subject of textbooks, but to distill it down to its essence, it involves storing energy for cells to use through an electron transport chain (ETC). This electron transport chain is a series of complexes that transfer electrons from electron donors to electron acceptors creating an electrochemical proton gradient that drives the synthesis of molecules that store energy in the form of highly volatile chemical bonds. But if we reach back to our recent discussion, what we see is that the very basis of our lives, and the foundation of every living organism on this planet, depends upon grabbing a few wee tiny particles out of the ethers as they literally blink in and out of existence.

If that isn't some sort of magical hocus-pocus, I am not sure what is. To this day, scientists argue about the origins of the universe and the origins of life. What is important, for the purposes of our discussion, is that both the universe and life as we know it *does* exist. And this universe, this reality, only exists because you take part in it.

Enter Andrew Steed. Wizard. Shaman. Soothsayer. Physicist (without the math of course). In this little tome of treasures, Andrew shows us the other face of magic. Beyond the quantum physics, beyond the cellular microphysiology, beyond the biochemistry — there is us. And every day, and in so many ways the magic of our existence surrounds us.

But as usual, Andrew does more. He pushes the boundaries by showing us that as in any relationship, the ultimate outcome is a result of all the forces applied in the equation. Life is not some predetermined movie script, already written in indelible ink in some book residing on some passing cloud, nor some weave already spun by callous Norns or Fates.

We have free will. We can invoke magic. If we invest our work with Spirit, we put forth energy. When energy is released into the Universe, there are consequences. They can be good, or bad, or deliver unintended results — depending upon the circumstances. But as Andrew demonstrates in this book, they are most certainly tangible shamanic results. This is precisely because they manifest as observable, concrete outcomes and events.

This is no idle musing. Stuff happens. In my life, there is much that has been understood only through the language of birds. Perhaps it is because this is something to which I am particularly attuned, or aware. It is truly no surprise that wisdom dropped like a dark feather on the light wind. The stories Andrew shares in his book, the magic Andrew shares in his book, was never something that was impossible for me. Improbable at times, yes. But impossible, never. But therein, betwixt impossible and improbable, lies the magic!

But magic does not manifest by appearance alone. Even as smooth as raven's gloss, it requires our attention and engagement. Like with Schrödinger's cat, we must be present in full authenticity and sovereignty to observe the feather. We are often quick to demand our hour upon the stage and brook no resistance to *our* soliloquy. And indeed, Winston

Churchill noted that, "Courage is what it takes to stand up and speak." However, he finished that thought by sagely observing that "courage is also what it takes to sit down and listen."

For others, it may be something else. There is a language of trees, and wind and wave and water, tide and tempest. Nature is constantly offering us the opportunity of communion. Whatever the call, there is no doubt, that if we pay attention and listen we can hear the strings being plucked. The music will call to us. It can bring us in and harmonize us with Nature and the orchestrations of the Universe. For in the true reality of the Universe, we exist among the interconnectedness of all things.

This is what Andrew Steed shares with us. In this book he writes it in the language of birds. And in particular, through the dark tongue of The Morrighan. Some are called into the sweet delight, and some are called into the endless night. Where you are called, is irrelevant. For all is interconnected. What you are called is likewise irrelevant. What is important, as Andrew teaches us in this book, is to have the courage to shut up and listen to the impossible.

Because we should remember:

Everything is impossible – until it is done.

Michael S. Fenster, MD, FACC, FSC&I, PEMBA
Faculty, University of Montana College of Health Professions and Biomedical Sciences
Faculty, University of Montana Missoula College Culinary Arts Program
The Food Shaman

WORD MAGIC

Words carry power. Some words bring up both the light and dark within our hearts. Some words can create emotions on a spectrum from wonder to fear. Four of these words are emblazoned on the front cover of this book — **Magic**, **Crows**, **Ravens** and **Death**.

Let's first explore the word "magic." For me magic is evocative and certainly stirs the cauldron of my thoughts and feelings. I have witnessed a thirst amongst society for that dazzling sparkle that enthralls and delights in what we call magic! There is a thirst amongst us, as we look to connect with something that is beyond the horizon of our mundane lives.

Magic is a safe word when marvelling at the exceptional talents of a sporting hero, for example - Lionel Messi - the footballer known as the little magician. The same applies to our favourite singers, from West End and Broadway shows and entertainers and artists from all walks of life. It also is a comfortable companion when gazing in awe upon a glorious sunrise, standing in front of a cascading waterfall, or looking out across the land from the pinnacle of a mountain. The thrill of experiencing something otherworldly, albeit extraordinary talent or a natural phenomenon, moves us to a place where we embrace the magic.

I, for one, love a magical story. Millions have fallen in love with the "Wizarding World of Harry Potter." So many children at the age of eleven yearn for their letter to arrive by 'owl' from 'Hogwarts School of Witchcraft and Wizardry.' It was just before his eleventh birthday when Harry Potter received his invitation to Hogwarts. I know my daughter was devastated not to receive hers!

Little girls dream of being a witch like Hermione, Luna Lovegood or Cho Chang. Little boys imagine they are like Harry, Ron Weasley and for some, Draco

Malfoy. And how many adults have a secret longing to be Dumbledore or Professor McGonagall.

If you head to Universal Studios in Florida to sup on a Butter Beer you will see for yourself the global appeal that has captured the world's attention. Each day throngs of people flock through the portal Universal has created — to be part of the magic.

I wonder how many of us have been enthralled by the unique perspective of the musical "Wicked"? I for one was entranced by Elphaba, the so called Wicked Witch of the West. In a refreshing look into this age-old story, Elphaba, the green witch, is portrayed as the heroine of the story rather than the villain. What a role reversal compared to the Metro-Goldwyn-Mayer film version of L. Frank Baum's classic children's book! I grew up watching the MGM version of the Wizard of Oz each year at Christmas time and the Wicked Witch and her flying monkeys scared the living daylights out of me!

In the musical, when Elphaba sings "Defying Gravity" at the end of act one, she stirs the wild rebellious spirit in my soul. As she rose up flying in front of my eyes, I felt myself growing ten feet tall, with a heart that knows without a doubt that I can be far more than I have yet dared to dream. She pulled at my heartstrings to fly higher than a shooting star.

And yet for a large percentage of the population, talk of wizards and witches, of magic and the unseen realms is 'safe' only when it depicts a fictional make-believe world and is part of child's play.

The thought of animals that can talk to us, and of dragons and fae wizards and witches is an accepted part of our collective consciousness when in literature and the movies.

However, can talking animals, magical wizards and witches be real in our world today? My answer is a resounding "yes" for in my life magic is part and parcel of the fabric of the world. It has been a constant companion as I have wandered the highways and byways of the natural wild world.

Magical encounters offer splashes of colour and an array of sparkling stories to brighten the darkest of days.

I believe that many people shy away from an authentic magical pathway because it is outside of their sphere of understanding. In the Western world so many people alienate themselves from nature by preferring to read about it, watch it on a large screen TV or play computer games where the lead characters go on adventures in wild natural settings.

Along with the stereotypical images of mean ugly witches and wicked warlocks we have certainly cast those who wander away from societal norms — who live on the fringes of the worlds — as outcasts.

I have discussed the role of the "Sacred Outcast" in my book "13 Steps to Bringing Magic into Your Life."

The key ingredient to '**belonging**' resides in our own heart centre. The only place we ever need to fit in is our own beautiful shining heart.

I do believe our hearts are the doorway to living in a magical world.

WITCH-PRICKERS

I am certainly grateful that I do not live in an age of witch-prickers and religious zealots who would have tortured the likes of me a mere three hundred years ago. Here in my heart home of the Kingdom of Fife, Scotland, lived many a renowned witch-pricker. One of the most notorious was the Reverend Allan Logan of Torryburn. Witch-prickers were men who used a torturous metal-handled tool with a sharp point at one end. They literally pricked a long thick needle into the skin of someone who was accused of being a witch. They were well rewarded for their services. The Reverend Logan was famed for his fire and brimstone sermons in which he would point at a woman in the congregation and cry "You witch-wife, rise witch from the Tables of the Lord." So confident was his manner that this aggressive threat often resulted in the accused jumping up and running out of the church. This was part of his proof that a witch had been denounced. The next stage was the confirmation by witch-pricking!

I have read that the success of the witch-pricker was accomplished by sleight of hand. A witch was discovered if the needle drew no blood once it had pierced the accused's body. A person might be pricked several times and bleed and yet on discovering a blemish, a mole or birthmark, the needle would be shown to draw no blood. The witch-pricker controlled the experiment using a retractable needle that never broke the skin. Other articles written on this barbaric practice say that the witch-pricker looked for these 'devil marks,' blemishes on the skin, to see if they were sensitive to pain. Then they would repeatedly prod the mark rendering the spot insensible and then declare that a witch had been found.

It is amazing how many men and even more women were condemned for being witches for their eccentricities, physical features and mental faculties throughout Europe from the 1200's onwards.

Any religious organisation that encourages separation through fear closes the magical doorways of the heart. Throughout the ages great prophets have walked amongst us inviting us to open our hearts to finding ways to love our brothers and sisters more fully. I have always found it interesting to note that one of the greatest of these prophets, who in my eyes was certainly a Wizard, is none other than Jesus Christ. In fact the Bible is a feast for magical stories!

CROWS AND RAVENS

In exploring these majestic winged ones, who have incredible intelligence, I want to look at how stories have shaped them and shed light in the darkest of places. For like many of the innocent women who were victimised by authoritative men including the legendary witch-prickers, crows and ravens have been victimised and also share that 'witch-like' stigma of being seen as dark malignant forces in the world.

This dark edge flows through poetry, art, films and stories. As recently as 2014 'Disney' released a fantasy action movie full of magic that highlights how crows and ravens are forced out onto the edge in the dark realms. The title "Maleficent" features a faerie woman who is pure of heart. Her name is Maleficent which means evil — someone who is harmfully malicious. This beautiful fae woman who is a Queen of her realm has echoes of the "Celtic Phantom Queen," the Morrighan. For when I look upon Maleficent I am in no doubt that she flies on the wings of the crow or raven.

Maleficent lives in a world of beauty until she is savagely attacked by a best friend from the human realm. She is tricked and maimed by a man she trusts and loves. He cuts off her wings, steals them and uses them to advance his own claim to be king. Yet her name is the one that means doing harm or evil!

Her sidekick Diaval is a raven, although I have to say it has some very crow characteristics. Maleficent transforms Diaval from raven to man and back to raven at will. She saves Diaval's life when in raven form and for this he offers to serve her. She asks him to be her wings.

Just as in "Wicked," "Maleficent" gives us a refreshing twist on a story, yet both of them reinforce the dark side of ravens, witches and the world of fae in the names that carry them — and names do carry power!

One final thought here — the irony of a needle, a witch and a prick to the skin. Maleficent is lambasted for the curse she places on the king's daughter Aurora: a magical curse that comes true when a single prick from a needle on a spinning wheel sends Aurora into a long-lasting sleep. Compare this with the persecution of the witch-prickers who plied their trade with no culpability. They were lauded as heroes while hundreds of innocent women suffered at their callous hands. Many of these women were denied a burial in so-called 'consecrated ground' because of the false tag of witch.

BLACK RAVEN WHITE DOVE

In the Bible during the great flood that cleanses the earth, Noah releases a raven to see if there is land ahead. The raven does not return. After a seven-day wait, Noah sends out a dove that duly returns. After a further seven days he sends the dove out across the sea again. This time the dove returns with an olive leaf. The dove is then sent out a third time and this time the dove does not return.

What I find interesting in this Bible story is that the black bird, the raven, is maligned as a scavenger, slurred with a tag of being unclean and a symbol of evil. Not only blamed for flying to and fro, which echoes comparisons with Satan, the raven is also berated for feasting on the flesh of the dead. This act of pecking the bones clean correlates with unbelievers who are condemned for deriving worthless pleasures from idle pursuits. Conversely the white bird, the dove, is celebrated for being a clean bird and a symbol of both the Holy Spirit and of peace — an interesting analogy of the dark black shadow and the bright white light.

In an Irish version of this tale I read that the Raven was originally white and the Dove was black. It was the wrath of God that reversed their colours in the world. I have never fully understood the idea of a fear-based angry Deity that punishes a being like a raven for being true to its nature.

If Noah had been Norse it would have been a very different story. Captains of the large Viking ships reportedly sent out ravens to see if there was land nearby. If the raven circled above the ship and returned to it then they knew that land was still far away. It was when the raven flew off in a direct line that the oars were pulled strongly following the direction of the bird's flight. Quite simply a raven would not return once it had found land.

SIMILAR YET DIFFERENT

Many people have difficulty in telling crows and ravens apart and yet there are significant differences that make them uniquely their own species. Very much like a royal oak differs greatly from a silver oak, as does a wolf compared to a husky or a leopard to a tiger, a raven and a crow have features and characteristics that are known only to them.

The first striking difference is size. The wingspan of a raven measures around 46 to 54 inches whereas a crow's wingspan is much smaller, around 32 to 40 inches. The voice of the crow is much louder with a sharper rasping sound to its song. The raven's tones are softer and more rounded than the crow's.

The other difference with their song is in flight. Crows like to party! They let their voices and wings out to play when flying through the air, while the raven soars silently on the wind. A raven also is known to do aerial somersaults and fly upside down which a crow does not do.

Crows are social beings. I loved living in Aberdeenshire at an old manor house where scores of crows would gather in the trees and serenade me each morning and throughout the day. Ravens on the other hand are often seen alone or in pairs.

Ravens have a ruff of feathers around their neck known as hackles which crows do not have. Their tails differ: a raven's tail is like a diamond wedge shape, the crow has more of a fan-shaped tail.

Both species are generally monogamous, mating for life.

These wise birds have been known to make tools and use them effectively. In cities where you generally find crows rather than ravens, the crows memorise the patterns of traffic lights. They know when to drop something for a car to crush so they can easily gain access to the tasty morsel inside. Better still they know exactly when to fly to retrieve their prize during the

changeover in lights when all traffic comes to a
momentary standstill!

MASKED MEN AND CROWS

Then there is scientific research. I do not agree with
Dr. John Marzluff's methods in organising students at
the University of Washington in Seattle to set about
and capture seven crows. However, I do find the
results very telling.

Marzluff was interested in expanding his research of
the uncanny ability that he had noticed in crows — the
ability to recognise the faces of individual researchers.
He was intrigued by the behaviour of crows that had
been trapped and tagged, later being more cautious and
much harder to capture again by the same team of
people.

He bought several identical masks which were worn
by the students as they captured and banded seven
crows on campus. When the crows were eventually
released he had the students wander across campus

wearing those masks that had been worn in the raid. The students did this for several months wearing these masks and walking set routes. What they experienced was that the crows harassed only those in the antagonistic masks that had been used in their capture. Students who wore other masks were left alone. Even when students tried to doctor their masks by wearing hats, they were attacked by the crows.

Now here is the piece that I love. The number of crows now harassing their attackers grew. The longer that time passed the more crows which joined the fray. Dr. Marzluff reported that two years after the initial assault on the crows he wore the mask and was chastised by 47 of the 53 crows he encountered.

The best is yet to come though. The research showed that crows passed information onto the next generation. When the original crows that had been captured were no longer alive, their offspring swooped in to harangue anyone wearing the mask of their parent's captors. The crows had passed the information on to protect their kin from those who would do them harm!

This study was done again using even more realistic masks with the same results in different areas of Seattle.

Many researchers attribute this ability to not only crows but ravens and gulls as well.

It is interesting to note the names we associate with groups of these majestic feathered ones. Many crows become a "murder." Some of the names I have found for groups of ravens include an "unkindness" and a "conspiracy." These names reek of the long history of fear and loathing towards them.

Loving our brothers and sisters includes opening our hearts to all beings who share this miraculous planet with us.

I have found human beings to be quite fickle when it comes to our relationship with certain beings on the planet.

A FEAST OF STORIES

In the British Isles and Ireland, there is certainly an ambivalence towards these two birds. There is a reverence to ravens with their royal connection to the Tower of London. And yet here in the heart of London's history lies a love/fear relationship.

Legend has it that Charles II insisted that ravens become a permanent fixture at the Tower during his reign from 1660 – 1685. However, in mythology the association with ravens and the Tower goes back to the story of Bran.

The delicious tale of Bran was first scribed by Christian monks and then translated into English by Lady Charlotte Guest in 1849. I love to read several versions of the same story to get a flavour from whoever scribed their interpretation of a much older story. We know that the so-called 'Celtic' tribes migrated through Europe before coming to the British Isles around 700 BCE. These colourful glam rockers of their time loved a great story. The bards and seanchaithe weaved epic tales and delighted in high status for their role as keepers of the stories.

In our society today we often relegate the storyteller to a mere entertainer for children. Yet when a silver-tongued chronicler weaves magic from an ancient tale, he or she speaks directly to the hearts of an appreciative audience. In such a space we encounter a mystical and spiritual passageway that bridges past-present-and future!

I have selected several raven and crow stories to share within this book, both my own stories of personal encounters, and wonderful folktales and myths that all provide food for thought.

My relationship with both Crow and Raven have been so life-affirming. I hope you enjoy the feast that I have laid out here and that each of us gains a deeper appreciation for these wise intelligent beings.

And as for death? I concur with the saying "Today is a good day to die." You may well have come across this wonderful pearl of wisdom before. Yet, I wonder how many of us have truly embodied this concept? In my experience so many people haven't because they fear death. With a deep-rooted fear of death, we miss the treasure that is inherent in this universal truth. For while we fear death we actually fear life. I believe that our lives are to be lived to the full. I am excited to share tools and concepts that will invite us all to celebrate death fully so that new life can sprout forth within and around us all!

BOTH A TRICKSTER AND CREATOR

I will be delving into the stories of Bran and the Morrighan to honour my 'Celtic' heritage. However, I am going to begin with a tale from a land that adopted me for seventeen years of my adult life.

I moved to Pennsylvania in the USA in 1993. I was intrigued by the stories of this land that many occupants described as a new place lacking the rich cultural story of old Europe. So I found myself immersed in the tales and medicine ways of the First Nations people. In the stories I discovered Raven is known as a magician, being both a trickster and the creator.

In the 'Celtic' tales we have no recognised 'Creation story'. It seems fitting to begin with one that is a transformational journey on many levels. In the beginning, Raven's song was more attuned to the melodies that flow from a nightingale and a lark.

Raven flew in a suit of pure white feathers with a grim resolve to set things right.

RAVEN SETS THINGS RIGHT

In the beginning all that could be seen was a deep soft darkness and then Raven opened its eyes — two glimmering lights piercing and perceptive to brighten up the world.

Raven stretched its pure white body and radiant white wings gathering the darkness with those powerful feather tips and beating it, packing it down until it was substantial firm earth.

Salty water licked at the earth which was covered in thin spindly trees. Raven watched as a large jagged stone and an elderberry bush played in the mud desperately trying to make people.

Raven was vigilant and its sharp eyes and sharper mind figured out that if Stone won this contest people would be cold, inflexible and enduring.

Raven fluttered down beside Elderberry and whispered "Pull power from your roots so you can push Stone over onto the people he is making."

Raven was excited to see Stone roll onto the mud-beings splattering them all, leaving Elderberry to infuse the first people with fresh sap. Raven was delighted as life flowed into the bodies of Elderberry's creation.

The people had sallow skin and weak frail bodies. They munched upon nuts and dry leaves cupping their hands and drinking the dark salty water.

Raven had come to set things right. Plucking a branch from Elderberry, Raven shook it with all its might until the leaves scattered, rippling life into the sea. Schools of multi-coloured fish flicked their tails and darted off through the water.

The people were delighted for now they feasted from the fruits of the ocean. Yet still they remained twiglike and sickly. Raven knew that only fresh water would quench their thirst and help them grow.

Raven was aware of a fresh spring that streamed from the earth in a far-off land. A well that was rich and overflowing with pure clear water had been cordoned off by the selfish guardian of this life-giving treasure. This giant of a man had built a lodge around the well to prevent anyone from tasting the fresh pure water hidden within.

Raven flew to the well and asked the giant if he was up for a visit. The giant was sceptical of this beady-eyed bird that had landed on his doorstep. However, he was bored and he craved a good story. He agreed Raven could have a slurp of water for a well-told tale. Raven promised a tale of wonder, magic, mystery and suspense. So the giant allowed Raven a taste.

The water was crystal clear, tasting like sweet nectar as it flowed down Raven's throat. "Enough" growled the giant as Raven guzzled more and more. "I said stop" yelled the giant. Raven's beak flipped out of the water with droplets spilling onto the earth. Letting out a massive belch Raven shrugged, looking apologetically at the red-faced giant squawking "I only swallowed a drop."

"Consider it your last" barked the giant. "Now entertain me with your story."

Raven launched into a toneless tale, he painted pictures in tones of dull grey and his long-winded epic lulled the giant into a deep sleep.

Raven tip-clawed to the well and gulped up all of the sparkling water until the well ran dry. Raven's body ballooned out making walking difficult and flight near impossible. Making sure the last drop was well and truly swallowed Raven made room by releasing an earth-shattering belch.

The giant jumped from his slumber and stared incredulously at the bulging belly of his sneaky guest.

Grabbing a huge club, the giant swung viciously at Raven's head. Raven ducked and then waddled as the giant lifted his club for another deathly swing. Raven's wings flapped for all they were worth and slowly but surely Raven's body lifted off the earth. Each wingbeat carried Raven closer and closer to the smoke hole of the lodge. The giant bellowed insults at Raven and shook his fists in a rage of anger.

Raven made time for a cheeky look and gave the giant a wide-beaked grin before getting well and truly stuck in the smoke hole.

Raven's belly was so big there was no way through.

Now the giant laughed. He scampered to gather green wood and he purposely fed the fire so that smoke billowed up inside the lodge.

Raven spluttered and choked, struggled and pushed. The smoke threatening to consume the stranded bird, there was a cracking and ripping sound as the lodge roof gave way leaving Raven to fly gawkily across the sky.

Dropping water upon the earth, out of Raven's beak flowed creeks and rivers, ponds and lakes, deep wide pools of pure fresh water.

The people cheered and danced in joy as buckets of water rained down upon them.

Raven had set things right. The people saw an instant change in Raven. For Raven's dazzling white feathers had been singed and were now a deep dark obsidian, as black as the world itself.

Raven wished for sunlight, for then people would grow strong and healthy. With sunlight they would see the hidden gems in the hard-earned black coat that Raven now wore. Under the bright rays of the sun they would glimpse hues of green, blue and purple.

Now Raven knew where sunlight was to be found. Through a hole in the sky lived the Sky Chief. In his lodge hung three large leather pouches where the sun, moon and stars were stored. Raven soared on strong wings through that hole determined to steal the light for the people.

Using deep magic Raven's body became a speck of dust which floated into the drinking water of the Sky Chief's daughter. Unaware that she had swallowed Raven, she delighted in finding her belly growing with a seed of new life. There were joyful celebrations when she gave birth to a bouncing baby boy with jet black hair and piercing eyes.

The boy was strong and healthy and within three days was walking on his own two feet.

The boy was the pride and joy of his grandfather. The Sky Chief boasted often that his grandson got his brains from him. "Just look at him, he is as sharp as a spearpoint with eyes as keen as a ravens."

The babe had a ravenous appetite. The Sky Chief was concerned he would eat them out of hearth and home.

To distract him from his constant feed the Sky Chief would let the boy play with his tools and treasures all except for the three large baubles that swung from the rafters of the lodge.

Raven was patient. In the guise of the boy he waited until a day when he had eaten his fill and then he screamed. He bawled and banged his fists upon the lodge floor. He constantly looked up pointing at the three bags that were above his head. Finally, his Grandfather, fed up with the constant howls, reached up and tossed the smallest of the three bags toward the eager-eyed boy.

The boy crowed with glee, tossing, rolling, whirling the bag above his head. The drawstrings were tied tight and the boy clawed and picked at them until he worked those strings loose. With a dazzling swoosh a stream of stars shot out of the bag and through the smoke hole in the sky.

The Sky Chief was furious to lose such a wondrous treasure and the babe was quickly whipped away from the wrath of his Grandfather and given copious amounts of food by a distressed mother.

Once things had settled down in the lodge, Raven again guising as the boy, began an incessant wail. The ear-piercing screech was accompanied by the boy pointing up at the two baubles above his head.

The Grandfather reluctantly reached for the smallest of the two bags and making sure the strings were knotted tightly he tossed it towards his shrieking Grandson. The boy's eyes twinkled in delight and his nimble hands went to rolling, swinging and playing jubilantly with the shining silver bag, all of the while working to claw and unpick the taut knots apart.

The Grandfather watched in horror as the boy unfastened the drawstring and pulled the bag open. A luminous glow followed the moon out of the smoke hole into the vast star-studded sky.

Once again the Sky Chief stomped his feet and shook his fists while the babe feasted in the comforting arms of his distraught mother.

For a third time Raven went to work on the Sky Chief in the guise of his Grandson. In a fit of tears and an ear-splitting scream the boy pointed at the last remaining bag of gold that hung above his head. The Sky Chief looked on in horror as his grandson worked himself into such a state. With his choking and spluttering the Sky Chief was afraid that his grandson was about to die. In his desperation to placate the child he grabbed the golden bag and after making a double knot and pulling it as tight as he possibly could he tossed the bag to the bawling babe.

The boy rolled on the floor with the bag; he tossed it high and shook it violently around his head. At every opportunity he clawed and picked at the strings. Try as he might the knot remained secure.

Finally, the boy stood and shaking off his skin revealed his true nature; he stood before the Sky Chief in the black-feathered cloak of Raven.

Raven snapped up the golden bag and flew with purpose toward the smoke hole.

The Sky Chief grabbed his bow and nimbly fitted a poisoned arrow to the string. His arrows had been dipped in a deadly liquid containing all of the sorrows of time. Flicking the drawstring so that the golden bag nestled safely around his neck Raven crowed "I am Raven, I make things right. I am swift of flight and more intelligent than all of you. I shall take daylight to my people."

The Chief pulled the bowstring and let loose an arrow just as Raven flew through the hole. The arrow whizzed high into the sky, missing by a whisker. A drop of poison fell from the soaring arrow and dripped onto Raven's throat. When Raven sang a victory song fleeing from the Sky Chief's wrath a rasping sound flowed onto the wind. Raven's song now carries the strand of sorrow which Raven sings so eloquently to release the abundant joy of bringing home the light.

Raven flew towards a village packed with people. Fatigued and hungry Raven rasped "I have brought you sunlight in this bag, please feed me fish so I may have the strength to open it for you."

The strange voice that Raven used made the villagers suspicious and they all turned their backs refusing assistance.

Weaker still Raven flew to a second village and was greeted by the same response.

Digging deep Raven flew to a third village where the response was "We do not believe in this sunlight that you speak of, however you are more than welcome to eat your fill of fish."

Raven gobbled down a basketful of fresh fish and then set to work loosening the bonds of the golden bag.

Raven, now refreshed, called to the people to close their eyes. Then with a peck of the beak the bag split open and a bursting light shot forth illuminating the whole world.

In the other two villages the light was so bright that some of the people dove into the waters and became the otters and beavers and creatures of the river. Those who rushed onto the land became rabbits and deer and creatures of the forest. The people who had fed Raven remained as humans. Before they had been pale and spindly. Now they grew strong and healthy.

With the gift of sunlight, bursts of colour sprouted upon the earth, trees and flowers reached for the sun and life flourished in the world.

HOW THE TALE RELATES TO OUR LIVES TODAY

Whenever I come upon a creation tale I am immediately drawn to ask myself "What am I creating in the world? How am I bringing my unique gifts to shine more brightly in the world?"

It is Elderberry that brings forth life in this story. In the 'Celtic' tradition this powerful being is connected to protection, vivid dreams especially in the faerie realms and it has powerful healing qualities, especially in removing negative energy.

The First Nations people of North America appreciated the magical qualities of all aspects of the elderberry from the flowers, berries, bark, leaves and wood. Tea from the flowers offers a myriad of healing remedies reducing fevers, relieving headaches and flu symptoms, aids itchy skin and reduces pain from sprains, bruises and rheumatism. It was also known to treat kidney and bladder infections as well as softening the skin and improving the all-around quality of the skin.

I wonder where we are more like elderberry and more like stone in our lives. Where are we flexible? Where are we in tune with our dreams? Where do we offer healing in the world on a physical, mental and spiritual level?

Where are we cold and inflexible? Who and what do we shut out because life has been hard? What pieces of our own story lay unresolved in our bodies because we have hardened our hearts toward the experiences? There is so much trapped energy in our own bodies waiting for us to remember, reclaim and reweave. I wrote a helpful guide to working with this medicine in "Powering Up Our Life Stories." If you have not yet read it I thoroughly recommend doing so.

A huge motif in this story is hoarding. Both the Giant and the Sky Chief have rich treasures that they try to keep hidden for their pleasure only. This begs the question – Where are we hiding our own unique gifts in the world? What rich treasures have we held back from our community that would quench their thirst and bring a radiance of light into their lives? Albeit your art work, your knowledge of plants and the natural world, your poetry, your mathematical mind, your ability to make things with your hands, your skills in cooking, storytelling, listening, unconditional love and the list goes on… I believe we are all inherently more gifted than allow ourselves to be. So many people settle in life, shying away from stepping into the fullness of their power whether from a fear of failure or success.

Raven has courage to fly beyond the horizon through the hole in the sky — The willingness to transform being rebirthed to support the highest good of all beings. Without light and water life cannot flourish!

What are we willing to rebirth in our own flowing waters so that the fire in our heart can shine more brightly? If we are not willing to bring our light to the world how will our life and the lives of all our relations flourish?

This leads us into transformation. Raven ends up looking and sounding different because of the major journey undertaken here.

What transformation are we willing to take to serve the highest good of all beings? Perhaps the vastness of Raven's vision to take on such huge challenges seems overwhelming in our own lives. So how about starting with something that seems achievable and building muscle in our mind, body and spirit. In this way we shift a small piece in our lives which gives us the confidence to shift a bigger piece in time.

The Sky Chief is tricked three times into giving Raven the treasured bags. I wonder where we are being manipulated in the world. A great question to ask here is; Where are we giving in to someone who whines loudly until we finally let them have their way?

Parents take note. Small children are excellent at playing the game of the bawling raven until they have you all tied up in knots!

The selfish nature of the two villages affects both of these two communities in dramatic ways. Where is our selfish nature having an impact on our family and our community to the detriment of all?

Power of the inquisitiveness of crow and raven in and on us all!

CHAPTER 3. MARKED BY THE CROW

DUN I

If you have ever taken the ferry across the Strait of
Iona from Fionnphort, you will know the delicious
treat in store for you waiting on the other side. Iona is
a magical isle, a thin place. I have had the good fortune
to make this crossing many times over the years.
Leading small groups of pilgrims to stay on the island
for several days at a time has had a profound impact on
my life and on theirs.

Away from the maddening crowd, and as some locals
describe, the "Excuse Me-s," lies a treasure trove of
wild land to explore. The "Excuse Me-s" I have been
told are the Tourists who flock over to Iona each day
and head to the Abbey for a quick sightseeing tour.
Once they have sated their appetite touring the Abbey
grounds they tend to head off to the Argyll, St.
Columba or Martyrs Bay for a cream tea or lunch.
Then it is back onto the ferry heading to Fionnphort
and off to Oban. The reason for the "Excuse Me" tag is

the constant questions of – "Excuse me is this where I get the ferry? Excuse me how much does it cost? Excuse me what time does the next ferry leave? Excuse me…….."

I think we all play the role of an "Excuse Me" sometimes in life. However, when we travel as a Witness rather than a Tourist, we enter a space to be in relationship with the land rather than zipping through the journey to get there and back again. It is in the present moment, exploring the margins of the world as a Witness, that magic happens.

It is why I lead people on pilgrimage. Being present with ourselves, the land and each other, away from technology, stirs the magic in our hearts. I have facilitated over fifty of these journeys, along with countless workshops, gatherings and retreats that take place outside in nature. Just being in the wildness, regardless of the weather that has blessed my path, has totally reshaped my life. I sat in too many classroom settings discussing our relationship with nature in the early days of my educational years. I, like the Ravens imprisoned in the Tower, yearned to fly free. It is a delight supporting others to deepen their roots in the sanctuaries of the natural world so that we can all learn to spread our wings and soar upside down on the wind as jubilantly as Raven!

The beauty of Iona is that it's only a short step off the tourist trail and it leads to pure solitude. I always enjoy the wending trail we take up the steep ascent of Dun I.

Dun I stands 101 metres, 331 feet, above sea level. It is not incredibly high, however the ascent involves scrambling over rocks which get slippery when wet. There is a marked trail at the bottom of the climb which peters out the higher you go.

Dun I is magical; I have climbed in the bright sunshine where the summit affords spectacular views across Mull and to Staffa, Lunga and beyond. I have also scrambled my way to the top in the mystery of hanging mist, downpouring rain and bracing winds. All weathers afford a magical experience when we open ourselves to the moment of the experience.

WELL OF ETERNAL YOUTH

Davy Kirkpatrick the Skipper of the Iolaire of Iona will proudly share that at the top of Dun I is the Well of Eternal Youth. Davy is part of the family that for three generations has taken people to the majestic cathedral of a cave on Staffa. Fingal's Cave with its basalt columns is a sight to behold with acoustics that stir the soul.

The name alone — Well of Eternal Youth — whets the appetite and paints evocative images of the faerie world in my heart. It is a pool of water that will not disappoint. I have met people who have been to the top of Dun I and totally missed the Well. When you discover it, it is a treasure worth savouring. From certain angles it is the shape of a heart. The southern approach to the well leads you to the large rocks that embrace the dark waters of this natural wonder. The way the rocks wrap themselves around the pool leaves you in no doubt that you are looking at a womb, an organic birthing chamber carved from stone.

ST. BRIDE

The well is dedicated to Brighid. St. Bride of the Isles 'bridges' aspects of the Irish saint with the ancient goddess Brighid, daughter of the Dagda. Folklore shares that St. Bride is of virgin birth, born through a noblewoman named Morna, who along with Dughall Donn, the son of King Hugh of Ireland, made their way to Scotland after being exiled. Dughall was accused of impregnating her. Morna died in childbirth and Dughall, denying ever having had a sexual relationship with Bride's mother, takes her across the Irish sea where they are shipwrecked on Iona.

Apparently Bride as a babe started praying in an unknown language and was marked by the Druids as being the child that they had seen in visions. They claimed a child of virgin birth would grow to be the foster mother to the Prince of the World.

Legend has it that she scaled the heights of Dun I to greet the sunrise and saved a lamb from a falcon, which duly perched upon her shoulder, as the lamb lay peacefully in her arms. Two rowan trees sprouted at the Well creating an archway which she stepped through into the waters. Through this vortex she was transported to Bethlehem and assisted Mary with the birth of her son Jesus. It was Bride's plaid shawl that Jesus was wrapped in which bestowed upon her the name Brighe-nam-Brat, "Bride of the Mantle." She stayed to breastfeed the babe for a year and a day until the angels transported her back through the vortex to Dun I.

WORDS OF POWER

On every journey to Iona I climb up with the pilgrims to connect with the waters of the Well at least twice. The first time we snake up the hill, making sure the head does not lose the tail of the serpent. It is not a race, there are plenty of stopping-off points as we saunter to the top.

We visit the ceremonial cairn that honours the ancestors and all who have climbed this way before; then we descend slightly to the Well of Eternal Youth. The Well is also known reverently as the Well of Age. I love that it stretches to both ends of the spectrum — a name that carries beyond the beyond, a true life-death-rebirthing name! It is here that we speak words of beauty to the waters. Having the courage to voice words of power directly into the waters of this ancient Well is a true gift.

"Water I love you, thank you on your beauty, your song, your gentle strength, your wonder, your pure vibrant healing powers. Waters of the Well of Eternal Youth, thank you on rekindling aspects of my inner child in the waters that run pure and free in me."

I always speak from my heart and encourage those who travel with me to speak from theirs. I often scatter rose petals into the pool and then I invite us all to look at our own reflections in this Well of Wonder. We then speak words of power to our own hearts looking into our own soulful eyes.

"I love you, I see you, I believe in you, I am worthy, I am blessed." Again vocalizing words of power that are ignited by the magical ingredient *feeling*, brings a deep sense of healing into our own hearts, flowing through our own being.

I then like to sing a Brighid song honouring both the Christian and Pagan aspects of the energy of this Brighid Well.

BRIGHID OF THE MANTLES

Brighid of the mantles, Brighid of the fire,
Brighid of the waters, born of the Dagda.
Brighid, Brighid, Brighid three,
keen your magic, birth your magic into me.

Bless me with your healing, bless me with your song,
forge me on your anvil, fertile rich and strong.
Brighid, Brighid, Brighid three,

keen your magic, birth your magic into me.

Cleanse me in your firelight, birth me in your Well,
weave me in the rushes where protection dwells.
Brighid, Brighid, Brighid three,
     keen your magic, birth your magic,
     keen your magic, birth your magic,
keen your magic, birth your magic into me.
(Lyrics from the CD Sacred Outcast).

IN THE BETWIXT AND BETWEEN OF A DARK MOON

The veil opened up for me when I honoured the sun
and the moon and the betwixt and between in sacred
ceremony.

I set off from the west side of Iona in the rich darkness
of a no moon night. It was a supermoon, I marvelled at
the sound of corncrakes, their calls, which I can only
describe as an electrical charge lighting up the
airwaves. It is unlike any other bird song I have ever

heard. Iona is the only place that I have heard the call of the corncrake and once heard it is never forgotten.

There is great liberation in climbing a steep slippery Dun without the aid of a torch light on a dark moon. There is magic in being the only person up and awake on an island as small and as mystical as Iona.

I made my way to the birthing channel, to this Well of Youth, Well of Age. After making offerings of rose petals and whisky and adding my voice in song to greet the breaking dawn, I stripped off my clothes and stood naked to greet the sunrise. I then slipped into the icy waters of the pool and submerged my body in a cleansing rebirthing ritual.

Wow are those waters cold! Standing arms aloft in the centre of the pool looking up to greet the morning sun with water dripping from my hair and skin was exhilarating. My heart pumped wildly in my chest and my Spirit pirouetted in sheer delight.

I exited the waters via the "womb in the rock" formation. I felt resplendent, shining like a newly lit flame, effervescent and totally cleansed. After drying off with my t-shirt, I quickly dressed and I wrapped my hooded cloak around me.

I love my cloak. My talented friend Andrea Linebaugh from Pennsylvania decorated it several years ago. The design is of a radiant sun on the back, multicoloured stars on the hood, and on the front a fiery phoenix on the right side and on the left a bold dark raven in a bright full moon.

I welcomed its warmth on this morning. My insides were a fiery glow yet my skin was all a-shiver.

I have been leading groups of pilgrims this way since 2002, however it was in 2010 that I first journeyed to the crown of Dun I in this way. There is an old belief in folklore that if you climb Dun I seven times, you will be blessed by good luck. I have climbed Dun I celebrating life-death-rebirth, bathing under the dark moon seven times in the last seven years. I certainly feel incredibly blessed to have done so!

This particular morning the sky was illuminated with vibrant pinks, tinges of purple and streaks of crimson in a pale blue greeting of dawn.

It was with a light heart and a bounce in my step that I left the blustery summit of Dun I and picked a pathway down to the village. I hadn't taken many steps when a feeling washed through me that I had done this many times before. As I looked into the clear light of day I was absorbed in this crystal clear memory. The startling recollection was seeing and feeling myself as a woman. There was no doubt in my heart that I had lived a life on Iona where I had clambered up and down this steep hillside many times before. I had entered the pool naked under both dark and full moons and like today Iona slept and the inhabitants were oblivious to my actions. I felt like a priestess floating down Dun I and my feet carried me into the small chapel in the graveyard of the kings that is dedicated to St. Oran.

MAKING RELATIONSHIP WITH THE LAND

Legend has it that St. Columba was trying, without success, to build a monastery on what is now the site of the modern day Abbey. Every day the walls were built up and every night the walls came tumbling down. One night a sea-spirit, a mighty mermaid, came into St. Columba's dreams and told him no stone would stand until he had made relationship with the earth. A sacred offering was needed and it was Oran who volunteered to enter the earth and consecrate it.

Oran was said to be of royal birth, a cousin of St. Columba. He was buried alive and for three nights and three days he lay entombed in the earth. Then Columba, wishing to look upon the face of his dear friend once more, ordered that he be dug up from his grave. When they uncovered the body of Oran his eyes opened wide and he spoke to the frightened monks stating "There is no Hell as you suppose, nor Heaven that people talk about." Columba then yelled for Oran to be once again interred in the earth.

This story has always rung true to me. The piece that really connects with my heart is the importance of making relationship with the land. Making a heart offering — honouring the land, the ancestors, all of the seen and unseen beings — is an act of making sacred, an act of making love. From scattered rose petals and drops of whisky to words of power and the gift of song, an offering presented in love and gratitude allows magic to take root and blossom in delicious ways.

I entered the small chamber of Oran's Chapel to the sound of birdsong and the bleating of sheep. A black cat was curled up on a wooden bench and watched me lazily as I stepped towards the altar to light a candle. As the flame burst to life I placed prayers of gratitude on the highest good of all beings — for vibrant health, prosperity, peace, understanding, tolerance and love — to ripple through the ethers.

I then left some coins to more than cover the cost of the candle and wandered through the sun dappled nunnery. I love singing up the sun for the whole world has an added hue that glimmers and shines. I noticed spiders' webs and an abundance of flowers peeking their light into a brand new day. I decided to wander the longer route to look out upon the diamond sparkles reflecting on the sea. It was a delightful amble along the coastal path toward my comfy bed and breakfast close to Sithean Mor on the west side of Iona.

MAGICAL NUMBER 9

On all seven occasions that I have followed this route through darkness into light, I have yet to meet any humans except those pilgrims who have since wandered with me. There is such a delight that tickles my soul knowing that Iona sleeps as I walk between the worlds of both an ancient and present-day medicine way.

As I came in sight of my bed and breakfast abode, I was greeted by the song of eight crows which sat scattered on telephone cables above my head. I counted them once, twice and to be absolutely sure a third time — there were most definitely eight. My mind went instinctively to "Where was the ninth?" Nine is the most magical number of all representing three times the three levels of being, the upper, middle and lower worlds, and however many times you multiply it by itself it will always, by adding the resulting numbers, equal nine.

I stood bemused for an instant trying to find the ninth crow. As my head scanned the crows above me back and forth along the telephone wire I kept glimpsing the black hood of my cloak that was sitting upon my head. It was then that I let out a hearty laugh. I was the ninth crow. I heard this message in the raucous song of the crows above me and within my own expanded heart. "I am the ninth crow!" It was deep magic. I felt it ripple through my being, whistling the song of the crow through my bones until it nestled in my heart. Here was a miraculous reminder that I have been marked by the crow. The magic of this intelligent being carries me to see into spaces between spaces on this mystical journey of life.

IN SOVEREIGNTY

Seven times in seven years I have stood naked in the Well of Eternal Youth. The number seven represents all of the directions — connecting that which is above, with all that is below, bridging the rainbow light from the East Gate to the West Gate, from the South Gate to the North Gate, to everything within, the Gateway of our Hearts. Each climb has been significant and though all are worthy of a mention I would like to honour the Morrighan, "the crow and raven queen," for her role in the fifth climb.

Five in the 'Celtic' world is the number of Sovereignty. It is where all the gateways come together to meet in the centre, where we all stand in our own world. In our centre, we are either in Sovereignty with ourselves, the land and each other, or we are in "Dominion over."

When in dominion over the earth, we parcel up the land and sell it to the highest bidder. We rape the earth for all that we can gain, poisoning her, dishonouring her and using her without a care for the other beings who share this space with us, without a thought for the generations yet to come.

Each of us contributes to being in "dominion over" in many small ways. These seemingly inconsequential actions have the accumulated power to create a wounded wasteland. For example, buying a cup of coffee. So many takeaway places use non-recyclable containers. Some people buy one of these cups on a daily basis. I don't drink coffee; my tipple is tea. I take my own tea mug with me wherever I travel albeit on a plane, car, train or when I wander on the land including to the top of Dun I!

Many people look to have a manicured garden and pour poison onto the earth to get rid of what they call the unwanted weeds. My partner Joyce will tell you there are no such things as weeds, only varieties of flowers and every flower has a faerie!

The list of how we fall into dominion over the land goes on and on. We also can do this with humans as well as other species on the planet. When in dominion over others, we refer to them as "lesser" beings for they lack our intelligence or social standing. Every time we treat other beings as less important than ourselves we enter into a role of dominion over. There are so many beings that are living lives that are controlled by others.

I wish I could tell you that I am always in Sovereignty; I am not. I know that I grow closer every year. It is a journey of self responsibility, an awareness of my true nature. For me it is moving the ideology of Oneness, whereby we are connected to all beings, from a head-thought to a heart-thought. There are many people on the planet who speak eloquently of how we are all one and yet whilst this ideology remains a thought in their heads, they stay disconnected from the source. I believe the key to accessing Oneness and Sovereignty is through thinking, acting and being in and from our hearts.

The purest form of Sovereignty offers freedom that comes hand in hand with the responsibility in honouring all of life.

THE FIFTH CLIMB

On a dark moon day in July I guided six other pilgrims to the summit of Dun I. It was an early rise to wander through the darkness into the light. It was a special climb as the six people with me were all couples from the USA. It was a family group, two sisters and their cousin were travelling with their partners. No moon day was July 4th that year so we embraced their Independence Day.

I offered a different way to enter the Well on that visit. Instead of peeling off one by one, each couple stepped into these healing waters with their partner. As the first couple rebirthed themselves together, the other five of us looked towards the rising sun lifting our voices to the brightening day.

We weaved with independence and freedom away from country lines and embraced these qualities in our own bodies. We prayed on a shift in global consciousness for all beings to awaken to Sovereignty.

After the couples had bathed each other and we had all taken turns showering ourselves in the Well, we circled up at the natural birthing channel forged in the rock. We made further offerings, gave thanks and shared our experiences. It was then that one of the pilgrims proposed to his girlfriend. I knew that he intended to do this upon the summit, however I thought it would happen between the two of them. Instead they involved us all, friends and family; it was an act of intimacy that we were all blessed to be involved in. In that moment I felt like I represented the global family as these two lovers exchanged vows of commitment. Tears of joy were shed and a ring placed on a finger that symbolised the intent to make their union sacred.

As the seven of us stood hand in hand in circle I felt like we were the ring that symbolised a sacred marriage with the land. We stood in that moment in Sovereignty with all beings. With my cloak wrapped around me, this ninth crow was part of a group of seven that represented all of the directions. The ring was a symbol of the sun and the dark moon, the balance of the feminine and masculine and of Sovereignty.

BLESSED BY THE MORRIGHAN

I am in no doubt that the Morrighan blessed them on this morning along with Brighid's healing waters. And of course the Crow goddess is an aspect of Sovereignty!

I have since been invited to officiate the marriage vows of this couple where the seven of us who made up that ring will be reunited with more friends and family. I know the crows will be singing and the ravens flying a celebration loop the loop on their wedding day. An auspicious choice for they make their vows when night meets day in the balance of the autumn equinox!

Before I share more of the Morrighan's story, I would like to explore Raven's role as the totem bird of these Isles through weaving the story of Bran and the Beautiful Raven.

FEASTING ON A STORY

I recall sharing the story of Bran with a group of pilgrims at Harlech Castle in Wales in 2005. A man who was not with our party overheard the tale and when I had finished he brazenly interjected that I had told the story incorrectly. I asked him why he thought that. He insisted that he had read the correct version and it did not have Bran saying some of the things that had spouted from his mouth in my version of the telling.

If he meant to phase me his plan backfired as I reminded him that our ancestors did not write these stories down, for a reason. Once written the story becomes fixed; the tales were and are always morphing to bring the mythic healing qualities inherent within them to the listeners. The core essence of the story, its heart, lives on through the ages. It is in the tweaking and poetic language that a skilled teller brings the tale alive and allows an audience to chew on the marrow and suck on the bones!

And a 'Celtic' story often has many bones to pick from. Quite simply the ancestors of these Isles believed that our days start with the night. One has to journey through darkness to find the light. The dark can be a scary place. It takes courage to step into the unknown. The ancient 'Celtic' tales pack a punch, they bring up emotions within us as both the dark and the light ride close-knuckled on the wind. The story of Bran certainly stirs the cauldron with pieces that were difficult to write and for sensitive souls will be challenging to read. However, it is our willingness to walk through the shadows that allows us to shine more brightly in the world.

I have honoured the core essence of the tale and have not balked in tackling some of the gory details. To do so would be to desensitise the story.

One last point that is important before launching into a 'Celtic' tale is to mention the names of characters. Many people get stuck when meeting the obscure names and spellings that are so often found in 'Celtic' myth and legend. It can be challenging to the point that the obscure names bar the way of the reader from engaging with the story, keeping them from entering the pool of wisdom waiting within. My partner Joyce always says flippantly "I call them all Dave!" I actually appreciate her candour here. When I first started delving into the Welsh Mabinogion and Irish tales of the Tuatha Dé Danann I would always pick a pronunciation that worked for me. Nowadays with the wonder of the internet I can research other perspectives on the correct pronunciation. However, it is important to note that the same word is often spoken differently depending on the dialect of a particular county. It is also important to note that modern Irish pronunciation is very different from ancient Irish.

The one thing I always do when sharing a story orally is to let the ancestors know that I am doing my best. I feel them cheering me on regardless of whether my chosen pronunciation is how they would have spoken it on the wind over a thousand years ago!

So I strongly advocate that you do not get hung up on the names, instead allow your heart to open to the pieces of the story that speak to you, for the brew is rich for those who are willing to taste it!

BRAN AND THE BEAUTIFUL RAVEN

When the long boats from Ireland approached the shores of the Blessed Isles, their shields hung upside down to mark that they had come in peace.

Their King Matholwch had come to seal terms of marriage to Branwen, daughter of Llyr. It was said that Branwen's beauty was beyond compare.

The High King Bran welcomed the Irish King and his retinue. He craved peace between the realms and he wanted his sister Branwen to agree to the match. He wished only happiness upon her and the decision was hers and hers alone to make.

She looked at the handsome features of Matholwch; he was beyond good-looking and his dazzling smile spun a fine net to catch his prize — Branwen was smitten.

Had she had an older head upon those pretty shoulders she might have seen that there was a weakness in his vanity — that such a man cared more for himself than a prospective bride. One wise woman commented that he was too handsome by far. Another argued that such a man might be easily led by a more agile mind. They both agreed that Branwen would rise to rule the land through him. Perhaps this was a good match and yet in their bones they felt a shadow lurking that screamed of disaster, treachery and death.

The prince of darkness, rogue of shadows and malcontent meddler Evnissyen had been away hunting and had missed the nuptials. His anger seethed inside, gnawing at his blackened heart. How dare his half brother Bran and brother Nissyen glow with satisfaction as they toasted his half sister's betrothal. Why had no one sought his permission for such a match?

Where Nissyen was the light of joy to brighten any occasion Evnissyen was the polar opposite, guaranteed to add insult to injury by fanning the flames of a fire of his own making.

In his mind such a slight could not be forgiven. In the height of his intense rage Evnissyen stole away from the celebrations to where Matholwch had stabled his prize horses. With the thrust and cut of his blade, consumed by blood lust, he maimed and killed the whole treasured team. He cut off their lips to their teeth and their ears to their heads, and their tails to their backs and wherever he could clutch their eyelids he cut them to the very bone.

Evnissyen stormed into the feasting hall dragging the head of Matholwch's mount crying "Come Irish King and be bathed in the blood of Sovereignty, hug me and we will be blood brothers, then let's feast on the meat that I have provided in your honour."

Matholwch grabbed Branwen and dragged her, more as a hostage than a bride, to his longboat.
Accompanied by his warriors and with a foul taste of treachery and the stain of deceit blessing his union, he set sail for home.

Bran was mortified and sent another of his brothers, Mannawyddan, to redress Evnissyen's horrific act.

A staff of silver as thick as his little finger and taller than the king himself with a plate of gold wider than Matholwch's battle shield were presented to the Irish King. Also horses of equal quality and number were brought to replace those so recently slaughtered.

Matholwch may have accepted these gifts as recompense if it had not been for his trusted advisors.
With the gifts harshly rejected, Mannawyddan

produced the ace from up his sleeve. He had an intricately carved cauldron carried into the hall and placed before the King.

"This is only a mere replica of what Bran holds in the Isle of the Mighty waiting for you to collect. He asks that you return with me and bring Branwen, so that this time you can leave our shores as beloved friends rather than flee as enemies. If you choose to come he will grant you a rare treasure, a cauldron that is the equal to this one in looks and yet unlike this one — it carries deep magic within it."

"Only the head of Evnissyen will grant peace between our nations" mouthed Matholwch, using words insisted upon by his advisors.

"That is not an option" placated Mannawyddan "however, indulge me so I might share the magic of this cauldron before it is so readily dismissed. This is a cauldron of rebirth. A slain warrior placed inside this vessel will emerge the following day to take arms once more."

"A warrior comes back to life?" queried a bemused looking Matholwch.

"In essence yes" replied Mannawydan, trying not to look dejected. Bran had instructed him to make the offer of the cauldron only if all else failed.

Intrigued by such a treasure thirteen Irish ships set sail to negotiate a peace settlement and bring home the magical cauldron.

The hulking figure of Bran towered over the assembly and his words echoed sombrely in the ears of all in attendance.

"I give this cauldron to you and your people as a token of absolute friendship and trust. I ask that in accepting this gift you will agree never to use it. This cauldron may awaken the bodies of the dead, however it will not ignite their hearts, their souls. The warriors that spew forth from this cauldron will be mindless, they will know how to kill yet they will have no knowledge of why they kill. To unleash such an army will cause great destruction to us all. I gift this to you to show that I trust you and that you may trust in me."

Such trust bore fruit and peace reigned in both kingdoms for a year and a day. It would have continued to grow if Matholwch's advisors had not poured poison in his ears.

During that year and a day Matholwch and Branwen's relationship blossomed. Matholwch was indeed easily led and to the chagrin of his council, Branwen's voice grew stronger, her influence showered over the court and the green land of Ireland.

Along with her meddling ways a seed grew in her womb. A son was born, whom they named Gwern. Branwen shone gloriously, a radiant presence to grace the darkest of days — and the storm clouds were gathering.

There were constant whispers that the family of Llyr and all of the subjects in the Isle of the Mighty were laughing at Matholwch. The insults that had born witness to his wedding day were slyly fed to the King until he grew resentful of the radiance of Branwen. Her light began to burn his infected pride until he agreed to do the bidding of his court and he consigned her to the role of housemaid.

She was thrown into the kitchens and forbidden access to her husband's bed. Cruelly she was banished from the presence of her son. Her silken soft hands became coarse and chafed. Her shoulders slumped and her heart cracked. She may well have crumbled fully if it had not been for the small ray of light that crept in through a slit in the kitchen wall. Each day she would sing to the sun, the flowers, the rain, the moon and the stars in the heavens. Her one companion in this time of suffering was a starling who would flutter by to visit her each day. She would feed the bird crumbs and in time Branwen's song enticed the bird to land on her outstretched hand.

She spoke from heart and shared her sorrow with her confidante. She taught this colourful winged one to speak her name and after 3 years she sent a message tied to the root of its wings to her brother across the sea.

With great courage and determination, the starling, buffeted by strong winds, made it to perch on Bran's broad shoulders. Thinking it was a speck of dirt, Bran brushed the weary bird from his clothing. His attention was drawn to the earth where the starling lay dying from exhaustion. Bran gently lifted the bird into his massive hands and he was startled to hear the name of his sister sung delicately on the breeze. His curiosity piqued, he looked intently upon the bird and noticed a small piece of vellum tied securely to its wing. With great care he removed the message and learned of the plight of his beloved sister.

He held the starling, echoing the songs that his sister had shared with her faithful companion, until the bird's strength returned and was once more ready to take flight.

Then Bran summoned his war council and a mighty force set sail to rescue Branwen from her captivity.

When the men of Ireland gazed upon the imposing force that sailed ominously toward them word went out that a forest was crossing the sea. At first they marvelled at the magic before their eyes. It was as if an island had sprouted on the waves. As the marvel came ever the closer they heeded Branwen's words, for she had said all along that it was her brother coming for retribution.

Sure enough, at the head of those tall masts stood the mountainous figure of Bran, his feet straddling from port to starboard, a look of pure contempt chiselled into his battle-scarred face.

Panic seized Matholwch's troops and his advisors cautioned him to retreat across the River Liffey and burn all bridges to slow down Bran's approach.

When Bran met the river he lay his body down from bank to bank so that he became the bridge for his battle party to cross.

Matholwch, knowing that he was no match for the might of Bran, sent an envoy of peace, offering to stand down as King and to give Gwern, Branwen's son, the throne in his stead.

Bran rejected such an offer based on Gwern's age. Although his name meant "old," Gwern was a mere boy far too young to be king.

So Bran was offered the kingship in trust for his nephew until he came of age. For the sake of peace Bran accepted these terms and a huge castle was built for him to honour his role as regent of Ireland.

Evnissyen insisted on inspecting the castle before Bran entered his new abode. On perusing the feasting hall Evnissyen was curious in regards to the bags that were tied to the rafters. He was told that each contained offerings of flour for their new liege lord.

Evnissyen reached up and grabbed one of the bags, feeling the muscular body of a warrior hidden within. Deftly he sought the skull and with his full strength he squeezed the bag crushing the bones of his foe between his fingers. He visited every sack offering the same treatment until they all hung above his head, limp and breathless.

He then sang heartily "There is in these bags flour of a sort; champions, warriors, attackers in battle, against fighters ready for the fray."

Bran was then invited to take his seat at the head of the table. His nephew Gwern took his place for the first time at court and greeted his kin. However out of ignorance he overlooked acknowledging Evnissyen by bowing to a distant relative before turning his attention to the Shadow-Weaver. Evnissyen's blood boiled in molten anger and when he stood before the diminutive figure of Matholwch's spawn he erupted. He swept the boy off his feet and flung him into the roaring flames of the hearth fire.

Gwern's death screams were shrouded only by the keening song of Branwen. By the time she met the furious flames that had consumed her son, all that was left were his charred bones. She desperately clawed at the licking blaze trying to grab hold of Gwern's grisly remains. Had it not been for Bran she would have thrust her self, body and soul, into the heart of the fire. She squirmed in his muscular arms until all fight left her quaking frame and her howls scorched the sky.

Pandemonium broke out and a wild savage war was fought between both sides. Matholwch knew his forces were doomed unless he broke his oath and unleashed the undead. He knew that he would have no control over these soulless creatures that gushed from the lifeless womb. His need, so desperate, led him to ordering that all of the slain be placed inside the cauldron for resurrection.

Now the tide turned and Bran's army tasted heavy defeat. As Evnissyen watched brothers and comrades in arms fall to this ghostly foe he felt his heart crack with the unlikely flame of remorse. Such a feeling was alien to his being; it led him to an unfamiliar crossroads where he put his tribe ahead of his own vain needs. A realization that it was his hotheaded reaction that was leading to the extermination of his kin, set his resolve. He swapped his garb for that of his enemy and lay his body on the blood soaked earth limp as in death.

At the end of the day when the war horns and clashing ring of combat were silenced, the Irish corpses were once again flung into the giant cauldron of rebirth. When the strapping figure of Evnissyen was hoisted inside he quickly went to work. He manoeuvred his long powerful limbs upon the inner wall of the cauldron and with all of his might he sought to break free. From deep within he found a primal scream to aid his body in splitting the cauldron into many jagged pieces. As the large vessel cracked, all of the contents, the slain warriors along with Evnissyen's beating heart, fell into a blistering fire. Evnissyen was consumed by the light of the licking flames, his screams eventually silenced by the raging heat that cooked his skin and claimed his bones.

When the mist cleared and the battle thirst was quenched only seven of Bran's retinue survived. On the Irish side there were five. Bran had received a fatal wound from a poisoned arrow and he knew that his days were numbered. He called his warriors to his side and instructed them to cut off his head and to carry it with them until they reached the White Mound, a sacred hill that stood by the river Tafwys in what came to be known as Londinium.

They were told to bury it so his eye sockets faced toward Gaul for then no enemy would ever conquer the land. He asked that they take a journey to Harlech and stay for seven years. He agreed to talk to them during this time. Alongside Bran's voice, they gladly listened to the songbirds of Rhiannon. The golden wrens of the goddess enchanted them in a world where time appeared to stand still, for during this journey Bran's companions didn't age at all. Seven years passed in no time and they were then instructed to travel on to Gwales in Penfro where they were told to tarry for four score years.

Bran told them that they would find three doors, two of which they were permitted to open. Bran made it clear that the third door faced the land of Kernow and it was to remain closed. He solemnly shared that the day they opened it they must make haste for the White Mound for the flesh would fall off his skull, his eyes would glaze over and he would speak no more.

The warriors delighted in the company of Bran along their travels. Before they reached Harlech, Branwen lay down to rest. Her heart split wide open at the loss of her son and the death of so many friends and foe. With no will to go on she welcomed the onslaught of pain that ripped her heart apart and she was buried on Yns Mon by the bank of the Afon Alaw.

Bran was as good as his word. His companions forgot that it was only his head that journeyed with them as they savoured the wise words that he spoke.

He shared how hatred poisons one's own heart before it ever inflicts a wound upon an enemy: how words carry such power and that to unleash them without thought can deal such a blow that leads to lifelong scars. He shared that some only put a person down and ridicule others because they are afraid of their own dark shadow. We seek to make ourselves look bigger by making another look small. In reality this shrinks and shrivels the initiator of the process.

He then spoke to them of love: how by opening our hearts we see the beauty that resides within all sentient beings. He shared that life flows in spaces beyond what the eye can see, that 'feeling' is the gateway to accessing magic, albeit through the love of strife or peace. He urged his companions to love for the sake of loving, unconditionally with every beat of their heart, for a person who loves will always receive far more than they ever give. He talked about our connection to all things and that one's soul is more expansive than the oceans wide and the rivers deep. He talked of flying free on the wings of death for the spirit is eternal — there is no separation — death is merely an illusion for there is no beginning and no end.

At Gwales in Pendro for four score years Bran offered wise counsel to his friends. This mystical passageway became known as the 'Assembly of the Wondrous Head.' It was Heilyn, whose name means 'to prepare,' who looked one day upon the door that was always closed and barred, the door that looked out upon Kernow. "Shame on my beard" he spat out one day "I would that I knew if by opening this door the words Bran has spoken will come to pass."

When he threw the door open they witnessed a new world looking back at them and their sanctuary now felt like a prison. As good as their word they took the silent decaying skull of Bran and buried it as a protector of the Isle of the Mighty upon the sacred White Mound of Londinium.

RELATING THE TALE TO OUR LIVES TODAY
You may be wondering where were the crows and ravens? The name Bran means 'Raven' and the name Branwen means 'Beautiful Raven.' This rich story was crying out to be told for not only is Bran's head the original symbol of protection for the British Isles, there is much to glean from the telling.

Branwen who is described as being beautiful beyond compare jumps into a relationship with Matholwch who is described as being beyond good looking.

I wonder where the illusion of beauty seduces us into making   decisions that do not serve our highest good?

Branwen is the beautiful raven. She ends up like the ravens in the Tower of London, imprisoned with her wings clipped.

Where do we feel imprisoned in our lives? Where have our wings been clipped and by whom? Are we ready to reclaim our wings and if so, where are we willing to soar with our newfound freedom?

I love the song of the raven and when I look upon this bird I see and hear beauty every step of the way, every beat of the wing. Some might close their ears to a raven's so-called coarse song, and see its large hooked beak and sometimes ungainly walk as being anything but beautiful.

For me this begs the question of "what is beauty and how do we find the beautiful raven within us?"

In the tale we soon meet Bran's two half brothers although Nissyen, whose name means 'Peacemaker' has a much lesser role to play in the story than Evnissyen, whose name means 'Strifemaker'.

Evnissyen feels slighted at not being involved in the marriage of his half sister and exacts revenge in a gruesome way. His temper consumes him and he causes hurt on so many levels, to so many beings. I personally found the scene where he attacks the horses incredibly hard to write. It is disturbing to say the least. His act of desecrating the horses cuts deep into my heart. Yet this attack also has a deeper meaning on the spiritual plane — other than the horrific torture and death that he inflicts upon them in the physical.

The horse in the 'Celtic' world represents Sovereignty, the goddess and as such, the land. We will address this in greater detail when we explore the story of the Macha. For now, I will say that Evnissyen's actions violently dishonour the sacred feminine and the land. He harms his half sister Branwen; she is dragged from the celebrations as a captive rather than a queen.

There are questions upon questions for us to find ourselves here. For example: where are we desecrating the divine feminine and our sacred relationship with the earth and all beings?

Evnissyen's half brother Bran is affected by his callous actions. As host, Bran is responsible for the hospitality and well being of his guests. He chooses to defend his half brother because Evnissyen is family. Instead of offering Evnissyen's head to Matholwch he offers silver, gold, horses and ultimately a cauldron of rebirth as compensation.

I see Bran's actions in defending his half brother as an act of enabling. Where am I mopping up someone else's mess continually in the world that enables them? How can I break free of this pattern?

The whole court is affected because of Evnissyen's choices. His uncontrolled rage and attack on the horses are the catalysts which poison his half sister's relationship with her husband. This leads not only to a loss of treasure in the kingdom and a loss of face, for their honour is all at stake here, it ultimately leads many to leave their home and lose their lives in fighting a war of his making.

He harms Matholwch who has brought his men across the Irish Sea in peace. Matholwch's honour is insulted here which is magnified because of the Irish connection to the horse and its relationship with the goddess. This violation of the horses eventually spills into the King's own bed with his rejection of Branwen.

There are always those who will exploit a situation and Evnissyen's actions allow members close to Matholwch to poison his ear. Without such an affront to their honour Matholwch's counsellors may have found Branwen more than a match for them in the politics of court.

I always say that "we are all of the characters in each story." We play out these roles to a greater or lesser extent. We all have a Nissyen and an Evnissyen inside of us.

We are all an accumulation of the patterns by which we live our lives. Unless we are willing to reweave these patterns we play out the definition of insanity — doing the same thing the same way and expecting a different result.

It is Evnissyen's patterns of jealousy, ego and repressed anger that allow his inner demons to explode yet again, leading to the murder of Gwern.

There is nothing wrong with anger. We all experience it in our lives. It is how we work with anger that is important here. The ability to release and transform is of paramount importance. When anger is repressed in our three bodies — the physical, the mental and the spiritual — and our hearts seethe with jealousy, we can end up poisoning our relationships with dire consequences.

There are so many delicious morsels from this story to whet our appetite.

Branwen's ability to talk to the birds is one of them. I will address this in greater detail later in the book when I share my own journey with the crows in India. For now, I will invite us to consider — where am I making the most of where I am in the world?

Branwen goes from high status and comfort to low status and perceived hardship in the confinement of the kitchen.

Challenging situations in life is part of the ride. When I remember to be as "the beautiful raven" in the darkest of times I embrace the magic. When I forget, I become consumed with the appearance of the mundane and instead of channelling my inner Nissyan my inner Evnissyan pours disdain into the world.

Creating a magical moment in the face of the mundane invites us to live brightly in the moment. Otherwise we can easily succumb to being stuck in the mundane tasks and inadvertently wishing our lives away.

Quite simply we can moan about whatever task faces us, we can desperately try to get through it, or we can sprinkle magic dust, igniting a fire of passion in our hearts and be present with whatever task we are undertaking. Just imagine turning up the fun volume in more areas of our lives! Imagine enjoying a tad bit more of our story each day. For when we are IN-JOY the most amazing magic happens!

In this story of the Mabinogion it talks of the 'Assembly of the Wondrous Head,' it does not go into the details of what Bran did or did not say. Therefore, I have looked to the story of our two Ravens, Bran and Branwen, and of 'Celtic' culture to pose a possible dialogue that is both wondrous and wise.

The head is considered to be the vessel of wisdom and the seat of the soul so I believe the dialogue that I have chosen for Bran fits in very well here.

I wonder where our hatred has and is leading us in this world? How are we poisoning our own bodies with resentment, suppressed anger, jealousy, while throwing energetic daggers at others in this world?

Where is our harsh tongue cutting our loved ones, our coworkers, our neighbours and ultimately our own hearts into pieces?

In the story Bran shares that people who love will always receive far more than they ever give. How does this resonate in your heart?

Bran also talks about our connection to all things, that one's soul is more expansive than the oceans wide and rivers deep. He talks of flying free on the wings of death for the spirit is eternal. There is no separation and death is merely an illusion, for there is no beginning and no end.

An interesting series of words that carry a profound message. A great one to ponder and to also talk with a loved one about. Will we fly free on the wings of death?

Finally, I wanted to remark upon Heilyn opening the third door. The company have been told not to open it and of the consequences of disregarding this advice.

In this instance Heilyn's decision frees the company to move on in their lives. It was always going to happen and it needed to happen for things to shift in their world. Interestingly Heilyn means 'to prepare.' His actions prepare the way for the group of seven to journey on.

I believe the importance lies in being able to discern whether or not to disregard advice. How will it impact our lives and the lives of those around us? And then having the backbone to take responsibility for the choices we have made.

I marvel at how the ancestral stories are still part of the universal fabric of our lives today. There are other nuggets hidden within this story. Have fun finding further treasures within a story that at its core is thousands of years old!

And remember to revisit these questions and thoughts. There are many here. In our 'quick fix' world we so often gloss over that which would serve us if we are only willing to step beyond the margins.

THE TOWER OF LONDON

To this day it is said that Bran, the raven, still guards the land. Bran in the physical form of the raven is a permanent fixture at the White Mound. This sacred hill is said to be none other than modern day Tower Hill. The ravens reside here today continuing an ancient role as guardians of Great Britain. It is prophesied that if the ravens ever leave — the Kingdom will fall.

Charles II and the subsequent monarchs have gone to great lengths to keep the ravens captive. Each raven has had a single wing clipped so it cannot fly away. These birds have lived for up to forty years in captivity which more than exceeds their life expectancy in the wild. But a longer life does not always equate to a better life!

As a human I yearn to fly. I wonder how many of us dream of having wings that would allow us to soar through the skies. These ravens are born with the gift of flight, it is their birthright and yet a huge piece of their authentic selves and their Sovereignty is stolen from them because of a deep-seated fear. The Tower of London's website refers to the clipping process as a painless one. I find that challenging to believe. Even if it were possible to complete the mutilation without any physical pain, at what cost to the emotional pain? If I was a raven, I would wish to spread my wings and fly in freedom to wherever my heart calls.

This deep-rooted fear of the Kingdom falling is also tempered with greed. For many people are enchanted by the spectacle of the brightly coloured Yeomen of the Guard, known in slang terms as Beefeaters and the close proximity that they are afforded to the captive ravens. The term Beefeater is bestowed upon these members of the Queen's bodyguard because up until the 1800s they were paid part of their salary in chunks of beef.

It is interesting to note that the Yeomen are the oldest Royal bodyguards and oldest military corps in Britain.

The twelve Yeomen at the Tower of London play a different role than the other members of the Royal Guard of their Regiment in that they are known as Warders. The reason that there are twelve Warders goes back to 1509 when Henry VIII left twelve of his Yeoman guards who were old and infirm to guard and protect the Tower. The role of the Yeomen was originally to guard the prisoners kept captive in the Tower and safeguard the crown jewels. However today their role is that of tour guides and also as a tourist attraction.

They stand alongside the seven ravens who are imprisoned there. These seven include the six ravens required by Royal Decree to keep the Kingdom safe plus one extra in case any of the birds do escape, which has been known to happen. A raven named Grog vanished and was last seen outside the Rose and Punchbowl, a pub in the East End of London in 1981!

In part the Yeomen are still re-enacting their original role. The prisoners that they guard today are no longer traitors to the crown waiting to meet the executioner. They are kin to the scores of ravens that used to gather of their own accord to witness the beheadings and feast upon the remains.

It is ironic to note that ravens are often condemned as being thieves who would steal precious jewellery and yet have now been assigned to guard the most precious of our jewels, the Kingdom and Crown itself. Their role as a tourist attraction brings the money flowing in and I believe the real thieves are the ones who have taken away their liberty.

In 2013 two ravens were killed by foxes as they were unable to fly away from the predators. This led to some changes whereby the current Ravenmaster clips around a third less of the wing than his predecessors. This allows the ravens to fly short distances enabling them to reach the roof of the Tower. However only one of the Ravens is given liberty to fly further afield. Depending on how the wings are clipped a bird may have more or less ability to fly. Apparently the one who is permitted to leave the Tower always returns, according to the Ravenmaster, and yet he also shares that he sometimes has to go and collect her!

Changing how the wings are clipped is a shift in procedures at the Tower. The Ravenmaster has observed that with a little more freedom of movement the birds are both happier and healthier. Isn't that the same for all beings? I pray that one day the name of Ravenmaster is banished to the archives.

I dearly hope that the day comes when the ravens at the Tower will be released from this imposed burden and given autonomy so they can choose where they would like to live. Perhaps this will allow Bran's head and Branwen's heart, the raven and the beautiful raven, to find their wings throughout the land aiding the return of many more ravens to our shores.

For ravens are nowhere near as common to see these days in the Isles as their cousin the crow. Why? Quite simply the raven was seen as a threat to livestock and Victorian gamekeepers went on the rampage successfully exterminating and driving ravens from the land.

We are blessed to see a gradual return of these magnificent winged ones. Some areas in the UK are witnessing ravens nesting in their counties for the first time in over a hundred years.

Haste ye back ravens — I for one will welcome your song and your presence in the Isle of the Mighty!

HARBINGERS OF DEATH

The shadow of fear surrounding crows and ravens extends well beyond these Isles. Because of their keen association with pecking the bones of the dead and their hauntingly beautiful song, these birds are often considered to be ill omens.

They are known as the ghosts of murdered people who never received a Christian burial, symbols of bad luck, symbols of vice, beings that are associated with death, bloody battle, tragic news, selfishness, conniving, slyness, greed, tricksters and also being damned souls.

That's quite a list to dump on any species!

The darkness has been stirred throughout the ages in poetic verse, none more so than by Edgar Allen Poe's classic telling of "The Raven."

Modern filmmakers have conjured morbid and horrific tales such as the 1994 Gothic horror movie "The Crow."

Many people have a deep-rooted fear of death and here we find the human fear projected onto these two cousins. Crows and ravens are known as the harbingers of death, for wherever war occurred, so the flocks of death-eaters would darken the skies.

Crows and ravens would flock to the battlefield awaiting the conclusion of the combat. The dead and fatally wounded strewn across the blood-soaked earth provided a rich feast. The dark horde would swoop down from the sky and peck the bones clean, the carnage of all who were slaughtered in fight.

In Ireland the goddess of war and battle, the Morrighan, takes the form of a crow or a raven.

She is painted in the tales as being wild, frenzied, a creator of violent panic. It is upon her fearsome face of destruction that her reputation seems to ride and yet this shape-shifter, who primarily appears as a scavenging crow or ragged dark raven, has a softer healing side. She is after all an aspect of Sovereignty, much maligned and misunderstood.

I will delve further into this aspect of Sovereignty anon. For now, I would like to challenge this frightful and fearful portrayal of the Morrighan.

She who is often tarnished with the brush of evil, sinister and dangerous, is a powerful woman who speaks her truth forcefully and clearly. She is a wild, free and untamed woman.

In the patriarchal world she becomes almost a demonic figure. She is certainly one who is painted in darkness. Is it any wonder that the birds associated with such a powerful deity became outcasts in our eyes?

It certainly seems that when death raised its head in the story of the Isles, albeit from the Black Plague, the

Great Fire of London and the Civil War, crows and ravens were part and parcel of the cleanup.

With many humans having a real fear of death, knowing that crows and ravens will swoop in, peck out the eyes, feast on the brains, before devouring all the flesh is disconcerting to say the least!

Unless of course we do not fear death. What if death is a gateway to a magical adventure? What if there was a global shift in consciousness in regards to how we view death? Surely by releasing our fear of death it means we can truly embrace life!

ASPECTS OF THE MORRIGHAN

Streaks of purple, blue, green, obsidian, jet and pitch-black swept across the blood-stained sky. Hundreds of crows, if not thousands, circled in delight in readiness for the feast. Victory howls echoed on the wind, the pitched wails of keening women pierced the air and silent screams of the slain warriors lingered long after the battle was done.

A raucous cacophony of song joined the symphony of death as the winged ones dove towards their prize. Sharp talons sunk into the flesh of the dead strewn across the crimson earth. Out of the murder of brothers and sisters, who were fiercely pecking the bones clean, a beautiful dark haired Phantom Queen appeared. In the flash of an eye where <u>one</u> had stood <u>three</u> dark figures strode across the field.

One of them hovered by the keening women revelling in the frenzy of the high pitched lament of their grieving song. She stayed awhile until the call of sinew, blood and flesh enticed her to dance wildly amongst the feasting horde of her black-winged kin.

Another of the war-weavers straddled the ford calling the lost souls of the slain warriors to her womb where she cleansed their wounds and slapped clean the stains from their linens.

The third, a tall, lean, striking woman, with high cheekbones and a mass of jet black hair, streaked with purple and tinges of blue, knelt on the blood-stained earth. She placed her palms upon the saturated soil, sweeping the land clean, soothing, healing and nurturing the fertile ground until new life sprouted.

Satisfied that her work was done she picked herself up, casting a single remaining black feather from her hair, and then she ran. Her feet glided across the land as she raced into the betwixt and between of a gathering fog. Sprinting and galloping, she frolicked in pure delight until the mist began to clear and she looked down upon a large dilapidated farmstead.

Inside the farmhouse a local chieftain Crunnchu lived with his three young sons. The boys' mother had died of a fever a year and a day previously on Samhain's Eve. Since then the farm had begun to slide into wrack and ruin. The retainers slipped away to find work elsewhere leaving a despondent Crunnchu to wallow in his misery. His sad and neglected children yearned for their mother's tender touch.

The crow-like figure of Macha fluttered into Crunnchu's life without a word. She had cleaned the kitchen, fed the boys and stoked a cosy fire in the hearth before Crunnchu was aware of her presence. However once his eyes fell upon the radiance of the dark haired beauty that had flown into his nest, he was smitten.

At first he thought it might be the spirit of his deceased wife for Macha was deathly quiet. After cleaning the house and putting the children to bed she lured Crunnchu into the bedchamber. If he harboured any reservations that she was real, the touch of her cool smooth skin and both her tenderness and wildness between the sheets left him craving more. Macha was a godsend. Crunnchu was transformed inside and out. He was not the only one. As the spark of his heart-flame grew so did the crops on the land. The cattle seemed to multiply every time he entered the field. Great prosperity rained down on Crunnchu and it wasn't long before a workforce flocked back to the farm. He marvelled at the silent goddess who had graced his life. She was an otherworldly creature who possessed the gift of magic. She was so strong for such a waif of a woman. And she was faster than his prize stallion. He looked on in disbelief when Macha raced across the land, outpacing on foot his three sons who urged their mounts on to no avail. Everywhere she went life blossomed. His children laughed again as did he. He found so much joy in the smallest of life's pleasures.

Then word reached Crunnchu of the upcoming Lughnasadh festivities at the Dun of the High King of the Ulstermen. He was excited to attend and Macha was happy for him to go. She was heavily pregnant and although she continued to tend the day-to-day running of the farm she had no interest in traveling North to be part of the king's assembly.

Macha had spoken so few words in her time with Crunnchu that when she spoke now he listened. "Do not speak of me. I will keep the fire lit for your return.

Promise me that in the meantime you will refrain from boasting about me."

Crunnchu nodded his assent even if his mind was thinking that keeping her a secret would be a challenge indeed.

A great feast with games and dancing, music and laughter ensued at the harvest gathering. Crunnchu jockeyed for position to watch the biggest attraction of all, the horse racing. As bets were placed and goblets upon goblets of mead consumed, the boisterous crowd cheered on their chosen steeds. The High King's horse proved to be the fastest of all and perhaps had Crunnchu backed it to win his words would have been left unsaid. However, as he was being ribbed by several intoxicated fellows who had put their money on the victor he bit back slathering "My wife could outpace any of these horses. Why she would make the High King's stallion look like an aging nag!"

The words of this boast spread speedily on the wind as man after man relayed the story all the way to the High King's ears.

The High King demanded that the braggart who had uttered this slur on his champion be dragged before him.

Crunnchu was terrified. His eyes looked to the earth and he stammered "I promised I would not boast of her yet, the words I speak are true sire, my wife could outpace any creature alive."

"If you speak falsely knave — then you will pay for it with your life. Guards, seek this woman and bring her before me."

When an entourage arrived at Macha's door she was stunned at the ultimatum delivered to her.

"Your presence is required before the High King. Failure to come will result in your husband being

shamed and killed for his deceitful lying tongue"
barked the brute at her door.

Macha revealed her swelling belly which was ripe and
ready to be plucked. She asked if the High King would
kindly wait until after she had given birth and then she
would answer to her husband's rash words.

Her request was harshly rejected as she was dragged
and forced onto a waiting horse.

When she rode into camp with her head held high a
buzz of excitement brought a throng of men to the
racing grounds — so many eyes gawking upon her.
She sought out Crunnchu's shameful face. He stood
sheepishly, under guard, by the High King's chair. He
mouthed words of apology as the High King
mockingly announced "So this waddling wench is
swifter than my finest mount, hey? Well get your sorry
arse on the starting line woman and if you fail to match
your husband's boastful words you can watch him
die."

Macha turned imploringly towards the crowd. She came face-to-face with harsh eyes and cruel jests. Each and every man jeered and mocked her, laughing at her ungainly gait. She winced in pain from the day's hard ride and pointed to her full belly. Her eyes full of tears, she pleaded for mercy; she beseeched just one man to step forward and stand by her side. Who had the courage to stop this humiliation? How could she race when new life was readying itself to sprout from her womb? The raucous rabble averted their gaze from meeting her eyes and closed their ears to her anguished pleas for help. Instead they rushed to place bets, shouted slurs and gulped down more goblets of mead.

Macha dragged herself to the starting line where the High King's horse snorted and stomped, scraping its hooves in the dust.

"I will race husband, so that you will live however — you will return to an empty cold bed and a farm once more cast in shadow" spat Macha towards her husband. Crunnchu cowered, still refraining from meeting her eyes.

The High King signalled for a horn to be sounded and on the blast Macha felt the crack of a stick on her backside. She darted forward stride for stride with the High King's horse. Neck and neck they ran. For a moment she surged ahead until the whip of the man driving the stallion behind her caught in the violet strands of her flowing black hair. Now it was the High King's steed that nosed ahead. Macha pumped her arms for all their worth seeking the wind beneath her energetic wings.

Froth and foam flicked onto Macha's face. The sweating beast that matched her stride for stride was being pushed, like herself, to its limits. With her last resolve Macha found an extra spurt that lengthened her gait and pushed her beyond all earthly speed. The horse's eyes rolled and it let out a snort as it pulled up lame. Macha threw herself at the finish line and slumped unceremoniously to the ground. Her thighs flushed with her birthing waters. She lay panting fiercely upon the earth and amidst the tears that streamed down her dusty cheeks, she let out a bloodcurdling scream. The onlookers gazed in silent disbelief, a mixture of awe and fear pulsating through their veins.

The rich harvest in her belly contracted and as she howled and grimaced pushed two babes, a son and a daughter, into the light of the world. The babies joined their wailing song to the heavy panting of their mother's breath.

Macha lay sprawled on the earth, blood and mucus staining her bony birdlike thighs. In the stunned silence of the crowd, above the cries of her children, Macha's voice rasped for all to hear.

"I curse you men of Ulster! You who all looked away when I asked for your help. You who laughed with scorn at my plight. All of you dishonoured me here today. I curse you! For nine generations, in the time of your greatest peril, when enemy tribes are at your gates, you will be incapacitated, you will fall to the earth and writhe in pain. You will be helpless, unprotected, defenceless. For five full days you will be inflicted with severe stomach cramps, excruciating back pain and a weakness in your knees that will leave you flailing around weaker than a woman in the throes of childbirth."

As the curse penetrated their minds and blackened the hearts of those present, Macha grimaced one last time, then took her last breath and passed into spirit.

Crunnchu crumpled to his knees. The babes were swept up and carried to the mourning father. A hubbub of chatter arose from the men who exclaimed fear and derision from the curse that was wielded against them. Some sought their winnings; others lamented their losses. All steered clear of Macha, diverting their eyes from her limp body as if a single glance would drive them to their knees squirming in pain.

Above the scene flew a flock of crows. Two willowy figures in black hooded cloaks keened vociferously, sweeping the Macha up. In a flurry of feathers where three women had been, one Phantom Queen stood tall and strong. And then she was gone. New life beat on feathered wings and the sky grew dark as thousands of crows cast the High King and his assembly in a long dark shadow.

HOW THE TALE RELATES TO OUR LIVES TODAY

I never tire of telling this story. It goes deeper within me every time I explore it. Macha's tale is so applicable to our lives today. The desecration of women and the lack of respect shown to the land scream to be heard here. It is an uncomfortable reminder of how the patriarchal world has raped the land. I believe that it is only by being in Sovereignty with all of our relationships, the divine feminine and masculine within ourselves, all other beings and the land itself that we can fully heal the global consciousness.

Macha is a horse goddess and as such she represents the land itself, she is an aspect of Sovereignty. As Macha merges with the Phantom Queen and stands in the fullness of her power she once more takes on the title of Morrighan. This crow goddess is often painted as the dark shadow which is revealed when the High King and the assembly are left standing in darkness at the end of this tale. In reality this shadow is of the king's, the court's and her husband's own making.

I believe the fear of the Morrighan mirrors the fear that is held of strong women who are direct and speak their mind in the world.

The crow goddess challenges us to face our fears. So many flee from the shadow of her wings. Those with the courage to meet her will be wrapped by those wings to encounter the darkness. It might not always be comfortable, and yet it's where transformation happens.

What if each of us embraced being in Sovereignty with ourselves, the land and other beings more than we have ever done before? I believe those of us who are willing to explore this road will take flight; by examining our relationship with the divine feminine we awaken ourselves to truly honouring the divine masculine. I believe through this process we will fly on wings of freedom bringing balance to the worlds.

I wonder how many of us are willing to examine our own roles whereby we are either in Sovereignty with or in Dominion over other beings? We play both of those roles to a lesser or greater degree. I wonder who amongst us will flee, who will hide, and who will step up to investigate the roles that we play here? And then who amongst us will go the extra step in shifting our behaviours to embrace being in Sovereignty more often in our lives?

LOOSE TONGUES AND INAUTHENTIC BEHAVIOUR

Macha brings magic into all areas of Crunnchu's life. He is charged with one task — to keep silent about Macha. At the races his pride leads him to breaking his oath to her.

I wonder where pride and our inflated egos lead us into making rash statements that cause other beings harm.

It is amazing how loose humans are with their tongues in this world. Finding someone who holds our confidences is a rare and valued treasure.

When Macha looks for help in the crowd they avert their eyes for fear of seeing the consequence of their actions, their own dark shadows. The interesting aspect here is that by pretending not to see, they create an even larger shadow for themselves. When we pretend in this way we create inauthentic relationship within our own being and in our relationships with others.

It takes pure moxie to stand up to the overwhelming majority when we know that an injustice is taking place. I wonder how many of us would have the fortitude to stand up to the King and the hostile crowd in a similar situation? Would we be willing to speak the lone voice of reason?

Crows and ravens have much to teach us. I respect their authenticity, their intelligence and their loyalty. I believe that the story of Macha and the lessons of Crow and Raven teach us all to take responsibility for our lives — to be the hope and the light of change in our world, to soar on outstretched wings, singing our truth so our song flows authentically into all of the spaces between the spaces of this world.

In the disposable age that we are currently living in, may we commit to be role models in honouring the land and all of the beings who share this precious planet with us.

CHAPTER 6: WHEN THE MOON MEETS THE SUN

MORRIGHANS CAVE

Davy Patton and his partner Cathy O'Neill, two delightfully vibrant souls, are the gatekeepers to the Cave of the Morrighan in Tulsk, Ireland.

Davy is amongst other things a talented artist. He wades into the peat bogs in the Emerald Isle and retrieves pieces of oak and yew. Peat bogs preserve the wood for thousands of years. His gift of carving comes to life as he finds the spirit living within the wood. With great skill he coaxes out pieces of Ireland's ancient story. If you ever have the good fortune to visit the Cruachan Ai Heritage Centre, you may well see the royal throne that is a shining example of his work.

He also carves replicas of the ancient Gaelic harps of Ireland and the Scottish Highlands. His attention to detail is astounding. The intricate whittling and precise decorations are a testimony to his respect for the master crafters of old. I have had the great fortune to see some of these works, including a harp, in person in the warmth and comfort of his home.

I remember him sharing that he would willingly carve the harp yet he would never string it. The three different types of strings that are plucked to bring music forth from his harps are made of bronze, silver and gold. The strings need to be cut a precise length which is why he would have no hand in it. The cost of the strings, in particular the silver and gold ones, mean that a slight discrepancy in the trimming could prove a very costly mistake.

I first knocked on his door in 2002 when I was searching for the entrance to the Owenygat Cave in the heart of the Rathcroghan complex. He kindly led me to the small dark opening in the earth that sits underneath the wild tangles of a hawthorn tree. The hawthorn is a sacred faerie tree; this one is rooted over the lintel, the vaginal entrance to this powerful descent into the womb of the Mother.

Davy invited me to knock on his door for a visit and a cup of tea, once I had resurfaced from my ritual in the cave. Meeting the Morrighan in her inner sanctuary is a thrilling and daunting experience.

In the last fifteen years I have entered this space seven times, once alone and with six groups of pilgrims. Each time I take a deep breath and make sure my roots are planted firmly in the earth. I make prayers and offerings in preperation before sliding on my back and bottom to plunge into the thick darkness that awaits below.

You have to shuffle and squirm your way through the small cavity that leads to both the light above and the dark below. Once navigated you emerge at the top of a steep narrow passageway heading into the pitch-dark earth.

At this point you can stand. I always ask for silence as we carefully pick our way down the uneven rocks to the sloppy wet mud that coats the cave floor.

Depending on the group we light our way with torches or we pick our way carefully over the slippery rocks in absolute darkness.

Either way the darkness beckons, for once below we switch off the torchlight and embrace the silence. I have journeyed in the cave, shared stories, keened, offered spirit songs and allowed the song that sings me in the form of Amrun to flow through my bones into the heart of this dark dank nemeton.

For a deeper insight into "Amrun" please refer to my book "13 Steps to Bringing Magic into the Mundane." A nemeton is a sacred space in nature that normally has water, a rock and a tree. This cave has all three with the Hawthorn tree guiding the way to rock, water and copious amounts of mud.

It is in this primal space that the Morrighan is said to drive her cattle through the Underworld. When the gateway of Samhain opens at the blood-harvest, her song flows richly onto the land.

She is a force to be respected and when her dark womb is entered with humble appreciation, she offers sacred cleansing: her methods of alchemy are not always comfortable. As the leaf mould rots and is decomposed into the earth, so the Morrighan picks the dead flesh away from the bone, consuming and purifying all. She is the harbinger of death, of life, of rebirth.

I have found that the Morrighan meets us where we are. So when we are rooted in fear of death, in fear of the dark spaces, we project those fears and our perception becomes our reality — she becomes the terrifying dark entity to fear and dread. When we open up to her as the protector of the people, as the guardian of Sovereignty, then we fly with the vision of Crow into the purification and transmutation of a bright new birth.

The Oweynagat Cave has spread her thighs many times over the years, swallowing me, rebirthing me, and inviting countless pilgrims into the sanctuary of her still fertile womb. On one occasion a man in his late 60's demonstrated strength and courage that impacted all in his presence. He had travelled to Erin's skirt-folds with his wife and daughter. He was someone who normally stayed home on rainy days and had already stretched himself outside of his comfort zone on several occasions. On a silent quest day, the heavens had opened and bathed the group in a refreshing downpour that would have had some running for cover.

The impression he left, from our encounter with the Morrighan in her muddy fruitful loins, was his dedication to go deep into the Underworld to remember himself. He has only one leg and his prosthetic leg was the old-fashioned kind that did not bend. He went both in and out using the power of his arms to propel him up and down the steep muddy narrow birthing channel. I worked energetically to support him every shuffle of the way. When we finally emerged into the bright sunlight tears spilled freely from all who witnessed his courage and determination —powerful teachings for us all stirred within our hearts. It brought me to a place whereby I examined my own personal courage trusting Spirit to guide my way.

MY FIRST VISIT TO THE CAVE

On that first adventure to meet the Morrighan in the darkness of her inner sanctuary many crows flew into the farmer's field to witness my descent. Interestingly they were still gathered in the field as I squeezed my way out of her magical womb to experience the welcoming light of rebirth. I lay for a while hugging the earth and let the tears flow freely as gratitude overflowed from my being. Thinking back to that moment I realise now that the keen eyes of the crows were watching me. They heralded a piece of magic that would unite the sun and the moon in me and around me, magic that has carried me well throughout the years.

In that moment, I made another offering of thanks, smiled at the crows that still lingered in my presence and then made my way to Davy's house. I was welcomed muddy boots and all, into his humble abode. He insisted that I leave my boots on as the stone tiles of his kitchen floor were cold. "What's a bit of mud between friends?" was his response to my insistence on removing them. Even though I have only seen him on subsequent visits to Tulsk I feel akin to this Northern Irish brother who has become a gatekeeper to a really special and magical portal in the heart of Southern Ireland.

Davy's name translates to "Beloved Skull" — a mighty powerful name for sure in the medicine of these Isles. The skull is known as the vessel of wisdom to the ancestors of this land. Skulls of a renowned warrior were a sought-out prize in battle. It was believed that the wisdom of the deceased was accessible to the new owner of the decapitated prize. It may seem gruesome to have human skulls for decorations in your home, however, I am sure those ancestors would look at our widescreen televisions with equal fascination and maybe bewilderment. Seeing a stream of gory images flashing into living rooms and bedrooms via a magic box (television), may lead to some serious head shaking in regards to our so-called advanced civilization.

The name Patton also means "Warrior of the town." So the full meaning of Davy's name is — "Beloved Skull, Wise Warrior of the town." His partner Cathy's name translates to "Pure Champion" — quite appropriate for the guardians to the Great Phantom Queen's Cave!

On my second visit to meet the Morrighan in the darkness of her cave, I was once again blessed with crows circling the raths (hill forts) that lead toward her loins. Again in the field the crows swooped down. On that day I took my mother who was in her sixty fifth year into the cave. She wept in awe of the experience. I am grateful to have shared such an intimate space with her in this lifetime. Once we climbed out I took the pilgrims to see Davy for a cuppa.

Above his hearth was an exquisite piece of bog yew shaped like an arrow tip. Yew trees represent life-death-rebirth which immediately connected me to Crow medicine and the Morrighan. This piece has the striking figure of Lugh, the sun god, etched upon its flesh. I yearned to take it home with me and at that time I did not have the money to make the purchase.

It was two years later that I ventured that way again. We were still in the season of Lughnasadh, the first harvest, in the 'Celtic' world. It was the last full moon before Samhain — Summer's End.

The pilgrims were all excited at the prospect of their descent into the Underworld and on meeting Davy. Once again the crows circled and I felt that it was an omen that I would be picking up that piece of bog yew with the stunning carving of Lugh. A muddy band of pilgrims crawled out of the darkness and with tears of gratitude we all placed our hearts on the earth in deep appreciation. Once we had gathered and made further offerings we wandered off to knock on Davy's door.

All eyes eagerly sought the wall above the hearth in Davy's kitchen hoping to see my intended prize; to our dismay the wall was bare.

A part of me knew that in all likelihood the piece would have been sold, yet the mystic in me felt that everything was aligned for Lugh to travel home with me. It was a day when the moon was full, when the sun god would stand in balance with the moon — I felt blessed by the blood of the Morrighan that was streaked in lines of mud on my face, had caked my clothes, and hung in globs in my hair. It was also my third visit into this ancient womb and it felt appropriate that the birthing would come with a mega blessing!

Lugh is the god of vision, who becomes King of the Tuatha Dé Danann in the epic story of the second battle of Mag Tuired. He goes to the Morrighan to get the blessing of the Crow Goddess with the Dagda who represents the land and Ogma the poetic warrior before going into battle.

The poet and bard within my soul saw my three visits to greet the Morrighan in her cave as making relationship with my own three bodies — the physical, mental and spiritual. I was also making relationship with the three aspects of the Phantom Queen. I felt deeply connected to the story of the Second Battle as if one part of me was the Dagda, with the fertile land being birthed through me, a second part was Ogma as I birthed my poetic self and a third part was Lugh birthing the High King within me.

I had a vision to work more deeply with the inspiration and creativity of Lugh as well as the life-death-rebirth and Sovereignty aspect of the Morrighan. I saw a clear way to do this working with this glorious piece of yew that the "Beloved Skull, Wise Warrior of the Town" had carved.

Bringing the intricate carving of Lugh on the bogwood home with me felt right! It was to be a transformational board to help others and myself step through our fears into the depth of our visions.

I had come into contact with a Fijian ritual the previous December that spoke to my bones in a very 'Celtic' way. It was at the Winter Solstice that I had been invited to put an arrow to my throat and walk into it. This sacred ritual empowers us to move through our fears into our dreams. It took place close to Tara Hill. I had walked the hill for three days connecting with this magical place of Sovereignty prior to volunteering to be the first person to participate in this heart-thumping ceremony.

The way this ceremony works is you vocalise to a peer group a thought pattern or behaviour that no longer serves your highest good — something that is holding you back from shining more brightly in the world. You then affirm the vision of what you are willing to walk into. As you release the old you prepare the way for new vibrant energy to come flowing through your being.

Someone then holds a board and takes up a strong position facing you with the board braced firmly in their hands. Placing the fletch end of the arrow upon the board you then take a strong stance as if you were Usain Bolt lining up in the steady position before the 100 metre Olympic final. The tip of an arrow is pressed to the soft piece of flesh where a tracheotomy is performed on the throat.

I stood in this position listening to a power word that I had chosen to support my journey. All of the group chanted in unison and the word "Trust" was ringing in my ears. I moved my arms up and down with strength and purpose three times. I lifted them high, as if I were a crow soaring on the wind. With each beat of my wings I breathed deeply and then on the third breath I walked into the arrow, breaking it in half with my throat chakra.

Jubilation flooded through my entire being! A huge rush of energy and the thought of endless possibilities surged into my heart! I was handed the three pieces of this shattered arrow, an anchor to remind me of the fear that I had broken through on this day. This process had certainly taken me to the root of my fear; it is an arrow for goodness' sake, digging into the flesh where a tracheotomy takes place — our beautiful voice box, the place where we are called to have the courage to speak our truth in this world.

Being a storyteller and speaker, I experienced this as daunting, real and ultimately magically freeing.

It was not about breaking the arrow — it was about being impeccable with my word, to make a public declaration of how I was willing to walk through my own fear into the brightness of my light. I knew instinctively that this powerful medicine way would serve so many people on the planet. I made a commitment there and then to seek out a teacher to help me to share this medicine with the world. It is so important to be the medicine, to study and sit with such a life-transforming ceremony. Rushing out and buying a bunch of arrows and having people walk into the points without knowing what you are doing could create chaos and do some serious damage.

As one hunter from Pennsylvania said to me when I pulled arrows out to work with them in the Valley of the Dead in Kilmartin, Scotland. "Andrew, these are **real** arrows."

As I sat with the expansiveness of this ceremony I was struck by the Crow/Raven medicine that goes hand in hand with the visionary work of the 'Celtic' god Lugh. The Morrighan teaches us to be impeccable with our word. She encourages us to be authentic, to stand in battle-truth rather than spin out in war-rage. For a deeper insight into the difference between battle-truth and war-rage please see my work in "13 Steps to Bringing Magic into Your Life."

The Morrighan also teaches us to be in integrity. Our words in this world carry so much **power**, more than I believe we have yet come to grasp. As I stood with an arrow at my throat there was a voice that whispered "you could die here today" and then I realised I would die that day — well a piece of me would anyway. For if I was true to my word, whatever I released would no longer be a part of my journey. As the Morrighan has shared with me many times "For something to live, something must die."

In 2014 she gifted me this phenomenal song that appears on my CD "Sacred Outcast."

MORRIGHAN

Oh Great Raven of the North
Harbinger of death for rebirth
Strengthen my battle cry
For something to live something must die
Morrighan, Morrighan, Morrighan.

Peck my eyes so I can see,
Consume my flesh come set me free,
Open my throat so I can speak (Ha)
Cleanse my bones with your powerful beak.
Morrighan, Morrighan, Morrighan.

Oh Great Raven of the North

Prepare my bodies for rebirth,

In battle truth and sovereignty Séa

Authentically with integrity.

Morrighan, Morrighan, Morri…Caw.

A RAY OF HOPE

As I stood in Davy's kitchen I stared up at the blank space where the mighty figure of Lugh had hung two years previously. My thoughts then went to asking Davy to carve me a similar piece. He picked up on the energy of the group who were looking with disappointed faces at me and/or the empty wall.

When I finally found the words to talk about Lugh they were tinged with a small ray of hope that he might have the piece tucked away somewhere in his house — Davy gravely shook his head.

"Such pieces come and go quickly Andrew. Two years is a long time, many lifetimes as I am sure you are aware." His face then lit up in an impish grin.

"However, I do still have Lugh — he's locked up in jail."

My face must have been a picture as Davy lyrically poured honey onto a deliciously magical tale.

"He's been behind bars since you left two years ago. I teach wood carving at a prison with IRA inmates. I took Lugh in with me to inspire them. As you know Lugh is the god of vision and hope. His fire has been illuminating creativity within those walls. Apparently he has been waiting for you to come and collect him. I'll go and release him if you like. You can call in after lunch and he will be waiting for you."

The cherry on top was still to be delivered as both Davy and I made the connection to Lugh's auspicious choice of timing. When Davy placed the board in my hands later that day he breathed deeply and his voice took on a richer lilting quality as he shared the fact that the IRA had recently chosen to lay down their weapons. They made a choice to walk in peace as

Lugh emerged from behind bars.

It felt like such divine timing that at the cave of the Goddess of battle and war, I was receiving this handcrafted gem of vision, hope, creativity and illumination — a 'Celtic' key to releasing the light.

When Davy placed this treasure in my hands I had goose pimples on my skin and shivers reverberating down my spine. I carry this physical board as it gifts those in its presence with a spiritual knowing in their heart-flames. There is great power inherent in both the light and the dark. In great gratitude for the medicine of the masculine and the feminine, of Lugh and the Morrighan, the Phoenix and the Crow/Raven, the light of the sun, radiance of moon and the dark fertile earth, the goddess and the god. In this magic and this medicine — they all carry me!

A BEAUTIFUL SONG

In 2013 I returned to India after a 26-year hiatus. It was a solo journey wandering the land for five weeks. I am so thankful to my partner Joyce for supporting me in my medicine walk. She knew how important it was for me to return to see how India had changed and how I had changed. My first visit to India in 1987 profoundly impacted my life.

In '87 I had set off from Plymouth with a backpack and boarded a boat to Santander. I hitch-hiked through Spain, the south of France, Italy and Greece. After working in a hotel on the Island of Paros in the central Aegean Sea, I boarded a plane bound for India. After three and half months travelling in Europe my life was about to change exponentially.

My first introduction to India shaped me in so many wonderful ways. It was a time when cell phones did not exist, nor the internet and in the south of India there were hardly any tourists. All of the Westerners that I had met on the flight to what was then Bombay and now Mumbai were headed north to Delhi, through Rajasthan to Katmundu in Nepal. That decided it for me — if the crowd was headed north, I was trekking south.

Spending three and half months in a land so outside my sphere of understanding was as much an inner journey as an outer journey. It helped me to meet myself and hear the beat of my own heart. Without the distractions of my life in the UK and with no one to please, I had a rare opportunity to be in touch with me. Wandering the land, being outside day after day, listening to what my heart was saying to me was a revelation. It was a spiritual evolution in my bodies — physically, mentally and spiritually.

It prepared me for leading pilgrimages later in life as this intimate experience with the land taught me how the land authentically brings up pieces inside of you. I faced myself in India and went through rites of passage.

I refer to that journey as going through expanded time. Three and a half months felt more like three and a half years. I sensed that this space gave me permission to find my authentic self and I grew from being a boy to being a man. It opened my heart and my senses to another dimension within me.

For my 2013 visit I planned to take the same route that I had wandered in '87. The best laid plans of mice and men! Spirit had a different idea for me. I was called to the sea. I found myself beginning my journey as planned, in Benaulim, in Goa. It was monsoon season and the roar of the sea was music to my ears. Then there were the crows. Everywhere I went they would fly to greet me. As I stood by the sea letting the song that sings me, Amrun, flow through my bones and into the waters, I heard the crows and the ocean's request. My route was changing. My journey was to head to Mahabalipuram on the East coast, around the southern tip of India where three seas meet at Kanyakumari and make my way to the west coast again through Gokarna, returning to Goa before flying home from Mumbai.

Each day I would sing to the sea and each day the crows would gather to sing to me. All beings have a song and all beings have the capability of talking and listening. Many of us humans have closed our ears to the voices of the natural world. Because it is not in our own language we regularly tune out the intricacies of these foreign tongues.

I am fortunate that my life is spent outside for so much of the year. It is not only going to a place that matters, it is how you go. Leading pilgrimages in the British Isles and Ireland since 1999, often three to four of these magical offerings every year, has shaped me. When we wander with soft eyes, as witnesses attuned to the natural world, magic happens. It is one of my great joys to lead people on these sacred journeys to make relationship with ourselves, the land and all beings.

Here in India it was the crows that called me to the sea. They accompanied me and guided me to Varkala, a place I had never heard of and had certainly not been planning to visit. It was their timing and the magical stirring that happened there that deepened the roots of Crow medicine within me.

Before heading to Varkala I stayed in Kanyakumari where I stood with my feet in the three waters that converge here on the waves. The Bay of Bengal, the Indian Ocean and the Arabian Sea flow into each other's arms. It was a throwback to '87 as once again I was the only westerner that I saw in Kanyakumari. I finally found a space to paddle in the lapping waves away from the throng of Indian tourists. I again weaved with Amrun to the song of the crows.

After planes, trains and buses this leg of my journey was by taxi. Arriving in Varkala the cab driver was keen to take me to the North Cliff; however I insisted I would go to the South Cliff. These two places are intersected by Papanasam beach which was to play a major role in my stay here. The South Cliff is deserted, the North is where the tourists head to the hotels and cafes, where street hawkers and artisan shops can be found in abundance. I chose wisely.

I stayed at an Ayurvedic retreat centre in a three-roomed spacious ground floor apartment with a balcony that looked onto palm groves, abundant flora and the cliff edge with steps leading down to the sea. Each day I was greeted by eagles and crows, butterflies and lizards. With yoga in the morning, massages available all day and a hearty Indian breakfast and evening meal cooked to order each day, I had found a small slice of heaven.

The crows had called me to this spot bringing me there three days prior to the dark moon. I discovered that there was to be a Hindu festival on Papanasam beach called Karkidaka Vavu. Apparently thousands of

Indians would descend upon Varkala to be part of the celebrations on what they called no moon day.

On the morning of the festival there was a buzz in the air of the South Beach Cliffs. Cars and scooters honked their horns and loud shouts of "good morning" greeted me as I made way to Papanasam beach. The closer I got the denser the crowd got. There were many stalls selling street food and traders with white linen cloths that were obviously part of the ritual wear for the ceremony. The going was slow as I ambled down the steep hill leading towards the beach. We ground to a virtual stop at the crossroads that led one way to town, one way to the North Beach and the third route to the sandy shore of Papanasam.

Stretching beyond where my eyes could see, the road from the town was full of people shoulder to shoulder bobbing up and down as they shuffled in unison, forever forward towards the beach. It reminded me of a snake as the cluster of bodies headed to meet the waiting Brahmans on the beach. Like it or not I felt myself being swept into the main flowing body as our side road merged with the snakelike procession before me. The last thing I wanted was to end up on the beach. I had an interest in observing this sacred rite, not gate-crashing it.

I was jostled onward forcefully but carefully I bounced my way across the width of the snake and just before the pathway disappeared to the North Beach, I stepped gratefully onto it avoiding the impending sand.

I looked to find a space to stand and watch the proceedings. I witnessed many Brahmans chanting what looked like a blessing on the numerous circles of people sitting on the sand. A multi-flamed lantern was swung before each of the participants who then lifted a banana leaf that was full of offerings onto their heads.

Again they went in snake formation where one by one they turned three times counter-clockwise before entering the churning waters and dropping the banana leaf and offerings behind them. They then submerged their bodies into the sea. There were several people on hand to help pull them out of the tumultuous waters. I was fascinated and wanted to know more about the significance of what was going on. I asked several bystanders, who merely shrugged. I asked at the nearby cafe and got no further in my quest for knowledge.

As much as I had wanted to observe what was happening I was not wanting to gawk and overstay my welcome. I thought about my own work and how I really appreciate it that most people who stop to take in what they are seeing quickly leave me, and those I am working with, to get on with our weaving.

I decided to continue on to the North Cliff now that I was on that side of the pathway, for returning at that moment looked quite the challenge.

I had made a promise to Joyce to connect with her to let her know all was well with me as I wended my way through India. So I sought out an internet café. They are few and far between now in India as it appears that everyone has their own cell phones these days with access to Internet. However, in 2013 there was one building with about eight terminals in it.

It was nice to step out of the heat of the day for a moment and before connecting to my email I asked the man behind the desk if he could share what was happening on the beach with me. He gave me a blank look.

As I wrote my email the man got up and left; a few minutes later another man entered and sat behind the desk.

When I looked up from the screen and met his eyes to say hello he gushed out the words "Do you know the significance of today?"

"No" I replied eagerly "I have asked several people and no one has been able to tell me."

He then looked at me intently with a bemused expression on his face and spluttered "I did not mean to say that, what made me say that? I…"

My response was "Well you did say it, so please tell me about what is happening on the beach today."

The man introduced himself as Ambu, which I have since found out means "water." He certainly provided a refreshing drink from the cauldron of inspiration and knowledge that day.

He told me that it was the Festival of the Crow, always celebrated on Karutavavu , which is no moon day, the dark moon, of Karkidakam, which falls in July or August each year.

A story flowed from his heart to mine "Before religion claimed its name, to be Hindu was to be born in Hindustan, to be born in this vast land we call India — the great goddess — Mother India. On no moon day the people gather to honour our dead, the ancestors.

These rites always take place by water and Papanasam Beach is an ancient gathering place for our people. "Pap" means sin. "Nassam" means destroy. People come to wash away sins, to clear negativity." My mind was racing with intrigue building upon every word.

He continued "Karutavavu Bali translates as the "New Moon Offering." This is an honouring time for our ancestors. In the month of Karkidaka the sun is in its own constellation. During this time the sun is the father and the moon the mother. They both reside in the same house connecting the paternal and maternal lineages. In this energy the dead souls gain strength in order to placate the gods so that they can cross over and achieve Moksha which means freedom. Their liberation from all worldly existence brings them eternal peace, and showers blessings upon their families."

"People fast after eating a bowl of rice the evening before. They rise early and make their way to the sea to where the Brahmans are waiting. The Brahmans work with mantras preparing people to go through this major cleanse. Fire is the truth — all is seen clearly through the fire. A fire is made using incense. There is no puja without fire. Puja is the process of being with Spirit — connecting with the elements. It is a spiritual celebration."

I sat hanging on his every word, my whole being vibrating from a place that resonated with an ancient wisdom bubbling deep within me.

"Darbha, a type of grass, cooked rice, pavithram, (rings made of Darbha) sesame seeds, cheroola (an Ayurvedic healing herb) and water are taken from bowls. These offerings are placed in a banana leaf. The leaf is wrapped and carried above the head until the person lets it fall behind them into the sea. This is a cleansing, a purification, all the negativity that has gone before them is now released. The person now dips their body three times into the sea. This is the final cleansing where all is forgiven by the gods. An offering of food is then made to the crows. The crows are revered, as they are seen as the souls of the ancestors."

His words flowed through my heart, through every fibre of my being. I felt pure elation and thanked him profusely for the story and then I shared a piece of magic with him.

First I shared that it was Spirit who had brought me to Varkala, to Papanasam Beach and then onto the North Cliffs so I could meet him and I believed totally that this was divine timing.

I told him "Each year the veil grows thin in the dark half of the year in what our ancestors in the British Isles and Ireland knew as Samhain." This is a thin time and in our tradition this is our new year celebration — for we begin in darkness so we can dance into the light. Samhain means "summers end" and throughout the Isles this was a major festival honouring our dead. A sacred rite called the Wild Hunt was weaved in the ethers. Not only in the 'Celtic' lands — this is something that connects the Germanic tribes and the Norse. In Britain, this land once known as the Isle of the Mighty, and in Ireland's fair green we, like much of mainland Europe, forgot our rich indigenous ancestry. However, the land remembers and the old ways have been kept alive through our stories and through pockets of wisdom-keepers stirring the cauldrons of inspiration and rebirth.

I have led this powerful ceremony in Scotland, England, the USA, Canada and Barbados and I have been to Jamaica to help sweep-clean the worlds and sing home the souls of the dead. That is what the Wild Hunt is all about, honouring our ancestors, singing home the souls, cleansing spaces, so that prosperity can flow for all beings. In the linear world Samhain is modern day Halloween falling on October 31st. However, our ancestors were not linear. This festival is a joining of the masculine and feminine. Some say Samhain would have been celebrated on the full moon and some say on the dark moon. I enjoy connecting with what I call the five days of Samhain. The full and no moon day leading up to the linear date and the full and no moon day after, in November. I look to lead the ceremony over either the full or dark moon during this time.

Like the Crow Festival in India, we build a fire where we place a 'Wicker Man' who is dressed in both masculine and feminine attire in the centre. The 'Wicker Man' is filled with all of our 'negative' releases so that we can be purified through the fire. Samhain is a fire festival, one of the four sacred gateways that mark the passing of each year. Building a fire is a reflection of the sun and honours its life-giving energy. So here we also have the joining of the sun and the moon in the same house — an honouring of the maternal and paternal lineages.

We leave food and drink at the Northern Gateway to honour the ancestors and the shining ones, the nature spirits of the land. This ceremony offers personal healing as well as planetary healing and serves all beings. In sweeping the worlds clean we enter into a ritualistic battle and here we work side by side with the 'Celtic' crow goddess, the Morrighan. She is an instrumental part of this medicine way."

Ambu looked at me thoughtfully and gleefully exclaimed "What we are celebrating today is our Wild Hunt."

"Now I know why I spoke of this celebration to you today. My grandfather is here. He is in Spirit. He nudged me when I came in to talk with you. My grandfather used to make puja for this festival, he worked the ways of the Brahmans. He is happy."

We both had tears in our eyes as we gave each other the biggest hug. I left that internet café with a bounce in my step and puja glowing in my heart!

Ambu had 'watered' my soul and I returned in jubilation to the Ayurvedic retreat centre with a clear intending of connecting with the Crow Festival and honouring the ancestors and all life.

I descended the uneven steps leading through coconut palms and badam trees until I was on the golden sand that stretches as far as the eye can see between the red laterite cliffs and the Arabian Sea.

I had gathered a banana leaf and five offerings for Spirit. I lit a fire to make puja and I sang the song that sings me. The varied lilting tones of Amrun flowed into the fire and into the spaces between the spaces as I prepared to cleanse and sing home the souls of the dead.

I danced across the red hot sand and waded into the incoming tide. I turned three times to release and I let go of the leaf behind me, plunging my body into the wild surf that pounded onto the beach.

I pulled myself from the salty water in total exhilaration. I found a rock to make offerings in gratitude to the crows and I climbed the worn steps to the sanctuary that awaited above.

It was three days later that I sat on my ground level balcony journaling my experiences of wandering into this magical story. As I scribed the words the story became much bigger. At least one hundred crows came flying into the palm grove garden of the retreat centre. Their song rang raucously on the wind. Feroz, the man who was the manager of the centre, came running out of his office to see what the commotion was and cried "horrible noise, horrible noise!" Immediately, with rippling laughter, I responded "beautiful song."

Feroz stood frozen to the spot. He did a double take as he looked up at the crows and over at me. I was sitting bare chested and for the first time Feroz saw the tattoo work on my chest. Emblazoned across my heart I have the Morrighan in her crow form. Feroz pointed at my chest and then up at the crows crying "Crow, Crow, you call in Crow?"

"Actually Feroz, it is the crows that have called me in." I replied in awe of the moment.

The crows indeed had called to me and I heard their voice. I made an oath there and then to return to Varkala to honour the Festival of the Crow and to bring a group of people to weave in the ethers with me.

Feroz had watched me as I had refused to smack the mosquitoes to death that had landed on my body the first night at the retreat centre. He had heard me ask them to leave my body alone and was intrigued that I remained virtually bite free during my stay at South Cliff.

Now surrounded by crow song he looked at me and a huge smile spread across his face. "You call in crow," he exclaimed again, shaking his head.

When I came to check out, Feroz gave me a huge hug and thanked me for coming to stay. He shared that he had never met anyone like me before. I smiled and told him that I would return and bring a group of people who shared a similar ideology.

THE TRAIN TO MANGALORE

Feroz kindly took me to Varkala train station on the back of his moped. He walked with me onto the platform and affirmed before leaving that this was indeed the platform that the Mangalore train would depart from; it was due to arrive at 9.15pm.

I gave Feroz a hug goodbye and I sat on a bench next to an Indian man to wait for my train.

Just before 9.00pm a train pulled into the station. It sat there for about eight minutes and then the man beside me caught my attention and lazily drawled "That's your train."

"No that's not my train" I smiled.

"Oh" he replied. For a few seconds he was silent and then again he drawled "That's your train."

I smiled politely and once more stated "No that's not my train. My train arrives at 9.15pm."

"Oh" he replied yet again "You go to Mangalore yes?"

"Yes I am going to Mangalore" I responded.

"Well that train is the Mangalore train. That's your train."

My head jerked instinctively toward the train and I got off the bench and strode over toward it. I reached for my glasses to read the words emblazoned on the carriage to discover that the man was absolutely right. This was the Mangalore train and as my brain comprehended that information, the train slowly pulled out of the station.

I dashed toward my backpack, grabbed my glasses and thrust them into their case. I heaved my belongings onto my back and started to run after the train. As I was sprinting down the platform I heard the voice of the Indian man calling after me and caught the word "glasses."

My heart leapt a beat as I realised with horror that I had left my glasses and the case on the arm of the bench. I didn't have a backup pair of glasses and without these I was in trouble, there was no way I could read anything without them. I turned and darted back to retrieve them from the outstretched hands of the Indian man.

I charged once more after the train that was beginning to pick up speed. I was grateful that the platforms in India are long. I was also relieved that unlike in the UK, Indian trains depart with many of the doors still open. I keep myself fit so I was fortunately able to edge myself closer to one of the open doors. I was running at full pelt and in the craziness of that moment I threw my day bag onto the train. My next move was to swing my backpack off of my shoulders and I launched that successfully onto the train too. Both throws were accurate and now all of my belongings were on the train.

If you could have heard the "Ahhhhhhh" screaming in my head it would have hurt your eardrums. It was with foreboding that I registered what I had done. My passport, my belongings and my wallet were all on the train and I wasn't. The train continued to pick up speed. I knew that I had to get onto the train. I bolted after it for all I was worth and then I threw myself at the open doorway.

I flew through the air and slid into the carriage on my belly. My glass case complete with my glasses fell out of my hand and bounced back toward the door. I lay sprawled on the floor, winded and bruised, grasping hold of my ticket in my other hand. There was a flurry of activity from within the carriage as a group of men came charging toward me.

"You crazy man, you could have killed yourself" screamed the first man who came to my aid. I slowly picked myself up from the floor delighted to find that I could move all of my limbs, nothing broken, just a few bruises to nurse. I quickly sought my glass case which lay open with my glasses intact resting inches from the doorway. I scooped them up and faced the crowd of interested onlookers.

"I made my train" I exclaimed jubilantly waving my ticket high above my head. As I went to bring my arm down the ticket was snatched from my hand and the passenger who had ripped it from me shook his head and exclaimed "This is not your train."

"This is the Mangalore train" I blurted.

"Yes it is" he retorted "This is the 9.08pm Mangalore train, your train is the 9.15pm Mangalore train, this is not your train."

The only thing I could think to do was laugh. It was an instinctive laugh, born from the relief of surviving flying onto the wrong train which I had known all along was not my train. As I laughed the whole carriage filled with laughter. At that moment the ticket conductor arrived and he began to laugh too.

He stayed with me until the next stop and then he escorted me off the train and found a guard who waited with me until my train pulled in a few minutes later. He then ushered me safely onto the train.

HOW THE TALE RELATES TO OUR LIVES TODAY

I have had some good belly laughs out of this story as have some of the audiences who have heard me tell it.

I marvel at how instinct takes over. I would admonish any of my loved ones if they thought about racing after a train and throwing themselves on board. How crazy is that! It really was an absurd thing to do. When I look back at it I have found the message of trusting my intuition. I knew it was not my train! I got caught up in someone else's story albeit the man was genuinely trying to help me.

There is much magic to be gleaned from our stories.

When and where do we spin out when offered authentic support?

Where do we go ahead and do something knowing full well that what we are doing is not the right thing for us?

When do we get so caught up in our perspective when trying to help someone we actually do more harm than good?

I once witnessed a group of people desperately trying to rescue a baby seal that had been abandoned by its mother. A boat was sent out to rescue it and then many people gathered around to comfort the pup. Numerous hands reached to pet this stranded being. When someone finally phoned a seal rescue sanctuary, the word was that the mother had not abandoned the pup at all. The cow seal was off fishing to provide for her young. Because the pup had been in contact with too many humans she/he would have been rejected by the mother. The pup was carted off to the sanctuary and a bereft mother was left searching for her only pup. Seals normally give birth to just one pup at a time; on a rare occasion twins are born. However, most cows do not produce enough milk to feed more than one young pup at a time.

The other aspect that I have sat with from this adventure boarding the train is that I could easily have died. Boarding a moving train in the way that I did was not smart. It made a great story yet it was a reckless thing to do. I believe in my heart that the Morrighan lifted me on her wings. I had made an oath to return to Varkala to honour the ancestors and celebrate the Crow Festival. In return she was making sure that I was still around to honour the oath.

THE MAGIC IS TANGIBLE

I had thought my daughter was going to accompany me on this journey to India and then she announced she was pregnant and the babe would be born eight months prior to our departure date. I had a few people interested in going with me and when I came to purchasing my ticket, I had no one signed up to join me. My partner Joyce who is so supportive of my Medicine Walk on this planet knew that even if no one chose to come with me I would be going anyway as I had made an oath and in July 2017 I *would be* in Varkala to honour that oath.

Joyce is amazing both in supporting my Medicine Walk on the planet and sniffing out the best airline deals. We are fortunate to live in a beautiful part of the world in the Kingdom of Fife in Scotland. We regularly have breakfast in bed and look out the window at the waves rolling in and splashing on our local beach at Lower Largo. We had feasted one morning and Joyce was surfing the net when she exclaimed that she had found an exceptional price on a flight to Mumbai with British Airways. She was able to get me an upgrade using some of my points which brought the price amazingly to what I had paid four years previously. With such a good offer she went ahead and booked the ticket. Just before she pressed to confirm the purchase she looked at me and said "Here we go, there is no going back now." She then pushed the button and at that exact moment there was a loud "caw" from an excited crow singing from our rooftop. The magic is tangible!

I did not advertise the details of the journey to India. I felt it was important to take this journey with people who have worked in depth with me before and had a strong pull to be part of this. So I shared snippets with people who had worked alongside me at the Wild Hunt or had been in Jamaica with me. A small group of committed souls stepped forward to be part of the magic.

One of those was my good friend Pat who has wandered many pathways in England, Wales, Ireland, Scotland, Jamaica and the USA with me over the years. She is a sprightly 75-year-old who is an absolute gem. We travelled to Mumbai together and then on to Kerala and chose a room on the third floor at the same Ayurvedic retreat centre that I had stayed at before.

Right from the word go I knew we were going to have an amazing adventure. When we stepped out of the taxi in Varkala I found myself face to face with a German man whom I had met four years previously. He opened his arms to give me a big hug and cried "It's the magic man, good to see you again!" Interestingly his name Ulrich means "Powerful Heritage."

I was really looking forward excitedly to seeing Feroz again and was a tad disappointed to find that he no longer worked there. Instead we were greeted by the friendliest smile of the new manager Anuraj and the wagging tail of a dog that looked like an overweight fox.

The fox has always connected me to the sun god Lugh in his trickster aspect and I had inner giggles of delight in finding out that the dog's name was Lucy!

I was aware that the meaning of the name Lugh which is the masculine version of the feminine Lucy, is "Shining One" or "Light Bringer." I was not familiar with the name Anuraj; I later found out it means "Enlightening, Illuminating, Brilliant and Devoted."

It was comforting to hear crows singing in the trees and see eagles soaring above the cliffs. Feeling the effects of a long flight and the shift in time zones I knew I would not be late to bed. After a tasty supper I was treated to a different kind of dessert which was as good as they come. There standing outside the office was Feroz. He beamed with joy in seeing me and my heart and smile reflected the joy right back at him. We embraced and he shared that he had not popped into the retreat centre for over three weeks, yet tonight something had told him he needed to swing on by.

He had been living and working in Trivandrum and had recently returned to Varkala to manage a new resort that was opening.

As we stood chatting, the largest frog I have ever seen hopped on by with a baby upon its back. I knelt and watched the frog as it made its way through the garden bringing two spider webs to my attention. Both a large and small spider were busily spinning away.

Standing with Feroz amongst these four other beings brought my mind to the number five. Here I was being greeted by the man who had witnessed the scores of crows flying in to call me to return and now these frogs and spiders large and small were there to welcome me also — five beings that held great significance as I listened to the magic dripping tangibly from the air. Five is the number that equates to Sovereignty, frogs represent transformation, healing, fertility and rebirth in my life and spiders represent weaving the web of life. And of course there stood Feroz whose name means lucky! The signs were pointing to an auspicious gathering.

Add to the mix the meaning of the first names of those who were called to be part of this weaving and we had gathered the Strong, Noble, Anointed One, Joyous and Little King of the Earth. There is such power in names!

Pat and I were blessed to have an outdoor balcony which was a welcome place to sit, relax and embrace the morning sunrise. It was a wonderful cool sanctuary to retreat to in the heat of the day and a majestic vantage point to watch the light show of the mating fireflies whilst listening to the song of the crickets as the betwixt and between met the darkness of the night.

Our first full morning we were blessed with the first crow visit outside our door. Many tall trees reached skyward in the retreat centre garden and one spread its boughs directly by our balcony. Pat was sitting outside journaling when I ventured out with a cup of tea. Her full attention was upon the crow that was perched in the tree no more that nine feet from where she sat. I had pushed open the door unaware that the crow was there, however my sudden appearance did not scare it away.

As I shared in Chapter One, crows recognise faces. After experiencing the upcoming interaction with this crow, I had a strong feeling that we met on my previous visit to this wooded glade.

I stood transfixed as the crow began to sing. I have heard crows sing many times in my life and yet I have never been treated to such a magical solo. There were three distinctive parts. Intermixed with the longer caw caw caw that is associated with crows was a higher pitched caw followed by a melodious trill. As our eyes locked on each other, the crow reached its head out and stretched its neck towards me with its wings reaching behind its body. For three minutes, four minutes, five minutes and more the crow continued to serenade us in such an intimate way. I felt the crow song vibrate through my whole being. I witnessed – seeing, hearing and above all feeling — the crow's eyes, beak and its harmonic melody reaching energetically from its elongated body to pierce my heart, connecting deeply into my soul. When the crow finally finished this ceremonial welcome and took to the skies Pat and I were left in absolute awe.

UNDER THE BADAM TREE

Halfway down the steep staircase that leads from the retreat centre to the sea is a unique space to sit and contemplate life under the shade of a badam tree. Built into a wall is a half-moon-shaped set of seats, a perfect place to convene as our group prepared to meet the magic of the Crow Festival. It was here that we journeyed to non-ordinary reality and I shared stories including an Indian tale of the Crow and the Peacock.....

THE CROW AND THE PEACOCK

Each day crow would fly to the zoo. There were always plentiful pickings left from the morsels of food dropped by the humans upon the earth. Crow watched as hundreds of people gathered around an enclosure housing the most magnificently decorated bird in the world. Crow loved watching the sun illuminate the rich colours that captivated the humans on a daily basis. Strutting this way and that was a bird of royalty. Such dazzling colours were revealed in full glory when Peacock lifted its long train of feathers and spread them wide. This act created a huge fan of colour, a plethora of eyes appearing upon its tail. Such a sight left Crow's beak hanging wide open in reverence.

After the people had left for the day Crow hopped over to speak to this dazzling bird. "Hey there dear Peacock" cawed Crow, "you are the most beautiful bird I have ever seen. Thousands of people flock to see you each week. When people see me they often shoo me away, sometimes throwing things at me in the bargain. I think you must be the happiest bird on the planet, oh I wish I was a peacock, I wish I was you."

The Peacock looked into Crow's alert eyes and sighed "There was a day when I thought I was the happiest bird to have graced the earth. It is true I am beautiful however, my beauty comes with a price. I am under lock and key, stuck in this zoo. People come to gawk at me, point at me, admire me and yet beyond these bars I see you. Each day I watch you fly free in the world. You sing gaily without a care and you laugh in the face of adversity. I have always thought you must be the happiest bird in the world. And the truth of it is I wish that I were you, I wish I was a crow."

HOW THE TALE RELATES TO OUR LIVES TODAY

This short story packs a mighty punch. We live in a world where so many people are dissatisfied with their lives. So many people with low self-image and low self-esteem.

There has been a lot of talk over the last few years about finding our authentic voice, our authentic self. It takes courage to stand fully in our own shoes as we walk the walk as well as talk the talk.

We live in a social media age whereby some people create false images of themselves to be seen in the world to generate "likes" on sites like Facebook. There is a lot of jealousy, personal attacks and competition as well as an addictive quality to social media sites. Some people spend hours creating virtual lives rather than experiencing the world beyond the walls that they hide behind. With images being flashed in our faces and people spending more time talking through machines rather than to each other, we are in danger of excluding ourselves from the natural world. You only have to look at children's toys in the western world to see the lights, the gadgets and hear the incessant noise from computer-generated voices.

I believe we find our authentic selves when we step outside into nature and allow ourselves to quieten our mind so we can go within and hear the true beat of our heart.

I wonder how many of us can comfortably put our phones, computers, televisions and other technological gadgets away and spend a few days without them? How dependent are we on them?

I grew up in a world in which children used their own imaginations to play. I have carried this into my adulthood where I still love to be outside in nature and play.

The Peacock and Crow story asks us to consider where we are in comparing ourselves to others in the world. It invites us to embrace the attitude of gratitude and see our glass as half full rather than half empty.

THE THREE STRANDS OF POETRY

As part of our preparation for no moon day the group headed to the South Cliff beach to sweep clean our own bodies. In the 'Celtic' tradition the Dagda has a harp, or some say a harper named Uaithne. This magical harp/harper when plucked/played had three magical properties. It brought the seasons into order, prepared one to go into battle and plucked the three strands of poetry.

In the story of the Second Battle of Mag Tuired, close to the battle's end, the Dagda goes with Ogma and Lugh in pursuit of his harp that has been stolen by the Fomorians. It is hanging on the wall in a banqueting hall where the Fomorians are feasting. The Dagda calls "Come oak of two blossoms.
Come four angled frame of harmony.
Come summer, come winter,
Mouths of harps and bags and pipes."

The harp comes to him and he plays upon the three strands to enable his escape. First he plucks the strand of sorrow, which brings the Fomorian host to tears of grief. He then plucks the strand of joy and the laughter rings out loud and clear until he plucks the strand of peace and they all fall into a deep peaceful sleep.

In understanding an indigenous 'Celtic' medicine way I have found the mysteries to be tucked in the spaces between the spaces of the stories. That is a huge part of a medicine way. It is by stirring the cauldron that the brew grows rich.

When I discovered that the three strands took the listeners through three different emotions I knew that it was time to lift the story from the page and into my own life.

What I learned was that the Dagda's Harp is a medicine way to put the seasons right within me. Each of us has blocks in our physical, mental and spiritual bodies.

I smiled when Davy Patton [see chapter 6] shared that he makes harps with three different kinds of strings — bronze, silver, and gold. I see these precious strings as symbolizing our three bodies, alongside the three strands that are part of the magic that is inherent in the Dagda's Harp.

Inside each of us are a myriad of tangles. All of our memories and the feelings attached to those thoughts dwell in the deepest recesses of our physical, mental and spiritual bodies. Some of those life lessons have been harsh and we have tied secure knots to try to keep the beasts that rage within from reaching our door. How confused we are in thinking that by suffocating and trapping our inner demons we can escape them. Stuck within they deprive us of life force. It is only in releasing and celebrating the death of that which is currently decaying in our bodies that we will find new shoots to propel us on wings of freedom.

NON-LINEAR

What I love about the ancient 'Celtic' tales is that they are not linear. So within one tale Uaithne is a harp and in another it becomes a harper.

One tale shares that Uaithne, the Dagda's Harper, has three children born through BoAnn. The first is named Goltrai who was born in great pain and he grew to be a Harper who weaved with the strand of sorrow. The second son was named Geantrai who was born in great joy and so went forth to pluck this strand to the full. The third boy was named Suantrai who was birthed peacefully into the world and shares this gift upon plucking the third of these strands.

The names of these 'Three Noble Strains' that are carried in the names of the Harper's sons all end in *trai*, which means "enchanter." The music of Uaithne magically summons deep emotions. It is a magical treasure that was an integral part of the Otherworld in these stories and I have found it to be an integral part of my life here in middle world on planet earth.

DEATH

I have worked with the celebration of death for many years now and I have found that most people balk at embracing death. Instead they pick the scabs and bleed in pain, poking at the wound that continues to fester in the state of decay.

In chapter one I introduced the indigenous saying "Today is a good day to die." I wonder how significantly life would change on the planet if we bought in wholeheartedly to this concept. In rejecting this universal truth and clinging to a fear of death, we place a huge barrier between existence and fully embracing living our lives on purpose.

With the Western world caked in fear, there is an emphasis on masking our feelings. Instead of experiencing a death fully and celebrating this natural occurrence, we have a tendency to block the flow of sorrow and push the death firmly into our bodies until it rots and spoils inside of us.

Whereas the raven and the crow fly in to pick the bones clean, humans tend to shoo them away. They are seen by many to be unclean. It is ironic that many humans favour sitting with the comfort of what they know rather than facing death's door and with courage walking through to a new way of living.

We are slippery beings and our fear of facing death coats us in the disease until we become numb, and our anger, frustration and pain is pushed into deep recesses as we desperately try to forget it. Many of us go into denial, many make death a crutch to hobble along on and many forget what the root of the pain is because it is buried in an internal graveyard of our living bodies.

KEENING

Keening is a lament. It comes from the Irish and Scottish Gaelic term caoineadh. It means to cry, to weep, to let go and howl wildly on the wind. There are references to keening recorded as early as the seventh century when the Irish monks scribed stories that had previously been part of an oral tradition. In the "Second Battle of Mag Tuired," we discover the following line "Brig came and keened for her son. At first she shrieked, in the end she wept. Then for the first time weeping and shrieking were heard in Ireland."

It is interesting to note that Brig, Brighid, is the daughter of the Dagda. She is credited with bringing keening to the world when her son Ruadan is slain on the battlefield.

In the twelfth century Cambrensis records that the Irish musically expressed their grief. They applied the musical arts to celebrate the funeral rites. The keeners were divided into two groups, one at the foot and one at the head. The chief bard began a low doleful tone which was accompanied by a harp. At the conclusion the keeners at the foot of the corpse began their lamentation, or ullaloo, from the final note of the chief bard's cry. This was then answered by the keeners at the head to unite them in a general chorus of the keening song.

The *Dublin Penny Journal* records in 1833 that in ancient times it was the duty of the bard that served the community of the local chief or noble to raise the funeral song. As bards went out of fashion this duty was entrusted to hired mourners. Through the passage of time the song came full circle and women took on the role that Brig had birthed on the battlefield.

There has certainly been a decline in the role of the professional keener in the Emerald Isle. In a recent BBC Radio 4 documentary Marie-Louise Muir explains how the Catholic Church in modern-day Ireland has played a significant role in diminishing the role of the keener.

Keening was viewed by the church as a pagan practice. It must have been challenging for the priest to have to cede power over to keening women during the funeral service. Up to the 1950's keening was common practice, however the pressure exerted by the church and the people's belief that this practice was part of a backward-thinking culture has led to this decline in keening.

Philippe Ariés, a French historian, writes that the during the 18th and 19th centuries there was a shift in how death was viewed in the western world. He shares how in the Middle Ages in Europe, death was a public ritual. There was a social aspect to the occasion which lent itself to a more open expression of grief. There was a wilder, more unrestrained communal experience that was cathartic for all involved.

The art of keening has been recorded in the practice of many ancient cultures. It was implemented in the early civilizations of Greece and Rome. Its roots can be found in the Middle East and Africa and when I lived in the USA I was taught a keening song by a First Nations elder.

Keening existed around the globe for a reason. It was and is a cathartic release. As Muir concluded in her documentary "Our grief now is too contained. We rely on taking anti-depressants. We go to a grief counsellor, but these people had a way of letting it all out, having a good scream, coming from the feet up, a good cry, a good purging."

This wild nature of the soul is where freedom resides. It takes courage to let the raw animalistic and primal self out to play. The depth of emotion that flows through authentic sorrow can be intimidating and incredibly scary for someone to witness.

SUFFOCATING OUR TEARS

It is why when someone lets the raw emotion of sorrow keen through them, that people often rush to fling their arms around them and stifle the tears. I believe this action is made from both love and fear. People rush to show compassion when they see another being in pain. However, there is a piece of fear there in witnessing someone in a wild throes of sorrow. It leads to a need to make it better, to try and take it away and ultimately stop the tears from flowing. When we do this we become an energetic dam that cuts the harp's strings leaving the song stuck in the shadows of sorrow.

We all face death on a day-to-day basis. In the indigenous world everything is life-death-rebirth. There are major deaths and minor deaths.

What is interesting to note is that one person's minor death is another person's major death. We meet the opportunity for death not only in a loved one passing over. We come face to face with death when we leave the womb. One life ends and a new one begins. All through our lives death comes knocking at our door. Death comes in many guises. The physical death of a loved one is probably the most obvious. Others include the breakup of relationships; this can be experienced through a child's eyes with divorce or from teenagers and adults who separate from a partner/husband/wife. Then there is the breakup of friendships to consider. Death is part of all perceived endings; moving house, moving to a different part of the country/world, changing schools, finishing school and/or higher education, changing jobs, the destruction of woodland to make way for new houses, a miscarriage, an abortion and the list goes on.

Whenever our paradigm is shifted we face an opportunity to shed and renew or to bind ourselves in the angst of change. There are many masks that are used to repel death — rejection, resentment, anger, fear, betrayal, abandonment, jealousy, guilt, shame, abuse, unworthiness, hatred, greed (or other dark strands in our repertoire of denial). Simply put, without a celebration of death, we remain bound to the rotten flesh of decay!

There are many who desperately cling to something that needs a release from death. I wonder how many of you have stayed in a relationship that was well past its sell-by date? Then there are those who have animals that are ready to go home who are pumped full of medication to give them one more week, month, year, here. The humans need to have the pet with them outweighing the animals needs. This happens with humans also who are tethered to life-support machines when they are so ready to go home.

HE/SHE COMPLETES ME

Relationships are a lot of work. They offer each of us a chance to polish our own rough edges as we rub up against each other bringing both our shadow and our light to the surface. What I have learned is that true love starts in our own hearts. The most important relationship for each of us to cultivate is the one with our own inner self and Spirit. The deeper my love is tended in a garden of authenticity — the more love I have to give — the more love I can openly receive. What excites me and gives me so much hope for our species is that each of us can expand our capacity to love. We are all capable of giving and receiving love at an even higher frequency than we have yet known.

A truth that I have gleaned from polishing my rough edges is that I "complete me," I am enough, I am worthy. As I bring my masculine and feminine energies to dance side by side in me I can bring my whole self to being in relationship with another. In essence, I believe I am the soul mate I was searching for.

When we look for this in someone else we step into a world of needing someone to complete us. When we find an attractive pebble on the beach of life and we believe we have found 'our one,' the feelings are off the charts. We are on an endorphin high.

A strange thing then happens. So many people look to mould this person into their perfect 'Hollywood happy ever after King or Queen.' Trying to fill a hole that exists in our own heart with the love sought from an external relationship will ultimately lead to our own insecurities surfacing. This creates barriers and knots that distort the love between both our partner and our inner self.

We can easily start suffocating the relationship as we look to change and own the other person. Strong attachments can come into play that create tangled cords when one of the parties chooses to walk away.

Quite often cords get slashed; large knotted fragments whip around in the ethers and either one or both parties can end up sucking from each other or energetically blasting one another.

It can be incredibly challenging for the couple to accept and honour the death of their love. Often one of the party, the one who has been ready to leave, is able to step away. However the other who has not come to terms with the fact that death is on their doorstep can easily pluck the strand of sorrow until they are drowning in a sea of their own tears — entrenched in the role of being a victim. I have witnessed people refuse to believe that they cannot rescue their relationship. They hope that the other person will change their mind as they desperately try to manipulate the situation so their ex can see them again.

For this person the grief is overwhelming. And because death is too hard to look directly in the face, they pick at the scab, opening the wound again and again until it is well and truly festering. In this betwixt and between state of life and death they can spend years, decades, a lifetime, mourning the loss of someone who has long since flown the nest.

LIVING DEATHS

These decaying times in our lives can be known as "living deaths." A living death happens each time we are unable or unwilling to embrace and celebrate the fullness of death. Another classic example is when someone has lost themselves in the title of their job. A person spends years devoting their life to their work — it becomes a sacred marriage. And whether they love their job or have just become so comfortable in detesting it, the moment that they face redundancy, the person often goes into a tailspin. Feelings of worthlessness, anger, shame and an assortment of other rotten cords rip at their heartstrings. Unless this death is acknowledged and celebrated, the person descends into a deep-seated torment. Here awaits a long drawn out journey of sorrow — a tragic living death.

SORROW

The vibrational string of sorrow has been well and truly plucked upon our planet. The vibration of sorrow is currently ingrained in the warp and weft of the collective. The loom of life is stained in tears, the land runs thick with the blood of our wars, the mental plane shrieks with the dark angry cries of fear. So many souls are stuck in existence-mode trying to get through their lives, so many souls trapped without bodies for whom ceremonies like the Wild Hunt and Karkidaka Vavu Bali are a welcome release.

Sorrow is an important strand on the Dagda's Harp. It rightfully needs plucking — however it is the first strand. The other two hold equal value and without them the sorrow pervades.

SORRY

My partner Joyce challenged me years ago asking why the word "sorry" slipped so easily from my lips. Her view then which I share today is that placing the word sorry unnecessarily on the wind adds more sorrow into the world. Once we have re-patterned our way of thinking we become acutely aware of how often the word "sorry" is bandied about.

Here is a classic example: before I left the gym the other day I zipped towards the solitary toilet on the ground floor to find it occupied. I waited for less than a minute and out walked my personal trainer. He had been in there for barely a minute. I knew this as he had been walking with me just before. I had only wandered to the coat rack to get my coat. His first words upon seeing me waiting outside the door were "oh sorry." A needless sorry for sure! So many of us have adopted this word and add it to our vocabulary without thought. Of course there are times to add a genuine apology when we have caused harm, distress or upset in the world. However, being sorry for something inconsequential that offers no offence is politely adding sorrow into the collective tapestry.

THE FIRST STRAND

Plucking the three strands is deep work and I advise working with someone who can hold the energetic harp while you immerse yourself in the magical music that plucking the strands has to offer.

When working with groups I always give a demonstration first. I open myself to Spirit and I become a hollow bone — I get out of my head and shapeshift into the Dagda's Harp. A Medicine Way requires a participant to become the elements, in this case to be the harp, the harper, the strings, the melody and the raw emotions that are part of the musical vibration of this transformative song. When I keen the strand of sorrow, my body, my voice becomes pure sorrow. This is not a mind journey where I <u>think</u> of sorrow, this is a heart journey where I <u>become</u> sorrow. What I know is that sorrow exists in us all. There may be knots from experiences we recall and others that have long since faded. There may also be tangles consigned to a box marked "do not open" where a dark traumatic story is trapped in a place that we have marked "wish to forget."

It is important to get out of the head and into the body for this is "heart medicine." It is not about going into the story and looking to remember the anguish or replaying the details of the story. There are times when I am called to keen because of a particular incident. However many times I am not cognisant of what it is that I am keening on more than knowing that there is sorrow to transform upon the first strand.

So I pluck this strand for all that it is worth. In the plucking I often feel like vomiting and I will retch several times as I spit up on the earth. I often need to knock and push parts of my body where I feel energy trapped. This is primal work and it takes huge courage to open our hearts to let the sorrow pour forth. However, the biggest part here is not to get stuck in the sorrow. That is where I see the global consciousness at the moment. So many people moan and cry and seethe in anger that consumes them. This pollution of thoughts, words and feelings spill out to be consumed by others who are already drowning in their own pits of despair.

When approaching the strand of sorrow, it is imperative to let go and fully <u>become</u> the sorrow. We do not relive our sorrowful stories, we simply allow the primal screams of past hurts to be released from the meat and bones that coat our bodies. I stress "being" the sorrow here as although our planet and all beings are caked in it, many people place barriers to fully feeling it when it comes to the deep cleansing work of keening.

So many people have become numb. To open our hearts to <u>being</u> the sorrow (that we have directly stored in our bodies through our own past challenges) takes huge courage. Add to this all of the war-rage that floats through the ethers from unprocessed anger, spiteful words, energetic arrows that are shot from jealous bow strings, wars on battlefields and the wars fought between neighbours, families, workplaces throughout the world. With all this heavy energy floating around us is it any wonder that our pores become clogged as we sponge up the sorrow on a daily basis?

As I have stated, keening is an authentic experience. If our fear blocks our pathway and we shed crocodile tears, then the opportunity for transformation is missed.

The key is to transform sorrow and celebrate death. To do this we must activate the second strand and pluck the string of joy!

THE SECOND STRAND

It is imperative to find the joy as we transmute the sorrow. Only by activating the joy can we find authentic peace.

I have watched so many people skip the second strand and head directly to the strand of peace. I have also witnessed those who skim through the joy, rushing right on through it.

I always preface this work by advocating that however long we pluck the string of sorrow, the string of joy must equal it, or preferably extend well beyond it. I push for elongating the song of joy for this is a surefire way to bring balance into the world.

Our world craves more colour, more vibrancy, more genuine laughter, quite simply – more joy!

Because the strand of sorrow has been so well plucked, the vibration is a much easier one for people to connect with. And because so many people have so much sorrow and unprocessed death stuck in their bodies many have a tough time expressing authentic joy.

I have discussed that the bridge to magic is "feeling" in depth, through my book "13 Steps to Bringing Magic into Our Lives." It is in feeling joy, in <u>being</u> the strand of joy, that the healing happens.

So the importance is tapping into the authentic feeling of all three strands.

It is time to open a new doorway to loving ourselves, each other and this beautiful planet by bringing authentic joy through us in celebration of death. The beauty of the three strands is that by plucking them fully, we open ourselves to an authentic experience. When the sorrow is real and we shift it, we create a huge empty space within us. A space that is ready and waiting for the joy to pour on in.

Having the courage to flood our bodies with pure joy is exhilarating. This keening song of joy ripples from our being and ignites a light of hope in the ethers. As the joy permeates my being so my heart opens and my body opens. I express this feeling both internally and externally in this physical and vocal dance.

The second string allows the full transformation from sorrow to joy to take place. It is liberating. When we are authentic with ourselves in the keening process the progression of this medicinal song is completely natural. Death is celebrated and as the harp rings true we have created space for a bright new birthing to take place in the worlds!

THE THIRD STRAND

In riding this wave, the celebration of death plucked from the Dagda's Harp, we find that the third string has a depth hitherto unknown to us. The tranquil peace saturates our soul. Every time without fail I am lighter, I have more energy, more life force because I dared. In honouring the strand of peace I like to go and lay on the earth. To place my heart on the heartbeat of Mother Earth. To smell her blood and inhale the fresh scent of her bones.

After the cleansing of keening it is important to honour and embrace the silence. For me my sight and my hearing is always heightened. It makes perfect sense as I have rebirthed myself in this way. Being with the silence in tune with the natural world allows the peace and gentleness to stir in all of our bodies, the mental, physical and spiritual.

The final plucking to activate the third strand is allowing our voice to express the peace through the song that sings us — Amrun. The gentle sounds that flow through my bodies are visible to a Witness holding space. They will feel the genuine peace emanating from the depth of my soul.

AMRUN

All indigenous societies have a form of Amrun. This is the name of a 'Celtic' medicine way. It means a place for magical chanting and it is the song that sings through us. It appears in text as early as the epic of the "Second Battle of Mag Tuired." For a deeper insight into Amrun please refer to my book "13 Steps to Bringing Magic into Your Life."

BEING THE WITNESS RATHER THAN THE TOURIST

We live in an age when so many people have taken on the role of Tourists. Many people exist in a quick fix, "give it to me now" voyeuristic state of being.

Leading pilgrimages has clearly illuminated the difference between a Tourist and a Witness. The Tourists are everywhere. They rush from site to site desperately trying to pack everything into their vacation. It is a photo-frenzy that is reminiscent of a quick fling, an affair with the land that holds no deep meaningful relationship. This quickie ultimately leaves everyone dissatisfied. It is a rush that feels good in the moment, yet has no lasting impact. The Tourist rushes off to get the t-shirt to say "I've been there, done that!"

The Witness settles in for a while connecting their roots and heart with the land. Photographs come much later if at all. It is all about being present which we are not when we constantly hide behind a camera lens or look at the screen of a phone. Whether we are approaching the landscape of the planet or the inner and outer landscape of our own bodies, the opportunity to be in relationship as a Witness or a Tourist applies. Making a sacred connection with the land feeds our bodies, feeds our soul. Just like when we choose to dine out or eat a meal in the sanctuary of our own homes, we either gobble down our food or we chew each morsel and savour the feast. We either give heartfelt thanks for the sustenance that lies before us, or we ignore the sacrifice of the plant and animal life that feeds our body. Eating is a sacred act — we are consuming another being's life force so that we may live.

The Tourist is in such a hurry to gulp down life's gifts that he/she wanders around in a state of permanent indigestion. Such gluttony has caused disease in all of our three bodies. It has led to so many people self-medicating in a variety of ways in order to get through their day. This denial of being in relationship in the presence of ourselves, others and the land causes prolonged sickness and is part of a slow problematic long drawn out death.

BEING HUMAN

When we make love with the land we enter into a sacred marriage. We take the time to breathe in each moment, opening our senses and making a relationship — connecting with all life.

The Witness connects the threads of the sacredness inherent in the land. The myths and legends of place feed our soul, the elements that greet us that day share different sides of a lover's face and the make-up of the landscape and the beings both seen and unseen offer insights into our own stories. This is the difference between the Tourist who is a "human doing" and a Witness who is a "human being."

The Witness goes to their own edge and connects with the bridge where magic truly happens. This bridge resides within us all; it takes us getting out of our heads and into our hearts. Bringing both the wisdom and knowledge from our heads and the strength and power of being in our roots into our own sacred centre — our heart!

HOLDING SPACE AS A WITNESS

Holding space is an art unto itself. It takes being present in our lives to be a Witness. When holding space for another being we connect the threads of roots and head to our heart. Our focus is then 100% on the being we are supporting. We become "An Sith" which means "peace and harmony." I always say that we become the green energy. Infusing the golden light of the heavens with the green energy of the earth brings a vibrant shade of green, the colour of the heart chakra.

You can find the details of this connection between heaven and earth which I call "Bridging the Worlds" in my book "13 Steps to Bringing Magic into Your Life."

Once you are in this space of being "An Sith," it is imperative to hold focus. The Tourist is constantly being pulled to the distractions of the world. The Witness is able to be totally present with herself/himself and the person whom they are supporting.

THE BRIDGE

It is important to note that the three strands of poetry are not plucked in isolation; there is a transitional bridge that is part of a flowing journey to weaving with the Dagda's Harp.

We do not simply throw a switch and move from sorrow to joy. There is a moment when the person holding space for someone keening will hear the two meet. Where one feeds into the other and for a short while it is impossible to know which strand is being played. A betwixt and between space, a magical moment where the strand of sorrow and joy and later the strand of joy and peace interchange until the old gives way to the new.

I love a bridge. It is in these spaces between spaces that big magic happens, that everything intensifies, allowing for major release and expansion to occur simultaneously. As the sorrow meets the joy and they infuse together, the joy expands and the sorrow dissipates. Now the keener becomes a beacon of light, the joy that ripples into the ethers helps both with the transformation of the newly released sorrow while meeting the thick wall of sorrow, anger, despair, frustration, resentment, jealousy and jagged hatred that permeates the planet.

In the next bridge joy meets peace. As the joy flows from us our cup runneth over. As we breathe into the peace I feel an alignment within my bodies until the peace flows forth within and then without as I add Amrun on the wind. The strand of peace is grounding medicine. A delicious way of being present and allowing space for new life to come flowing through.

DOCTORS, NURSES AND HEALTH CARE WORKERS

When my good friends Dr. Michael Fenster and his wife Jennifer were first introduced to this keening practice, they both expressed how they had a metallic taste in their mouth. It was as if they were spitting up blood. Mike is a gourmet chef and a heart surgeon and Jennifer was a nurse.

I remember saying something like "That's because you are both coated in death." Hospital workers who face physical death on a daily basis are going to pick up buckets of sorrow. One major piece is the unresolved feelings that flow from the families who are having the hardest time letting go of loved ones. Combine this with the health professional's own feelings that are wrapped up in losing a patient and the result is a layering of death that coats up over the years.

Mike and Jennifer both agreed that this way of keening ought to be available in all hospitals and care homes. They saw the intrinsic value in this form of release and renewal for all of the health care workers, let alone the grieving families.

I would go further than that and say that there is value in bringing this medicine into schools so that our youth can transform such shadows of unworthiness, pain and loneliness and build muscle in being in joy and knowing peace.

The beauty of plucking the Dagda's Harp is to cleanse our own tangled lines while also working with the sorrow that has been dumped on us or that we have inhaled from others that have crossed our path.

I have found that weaving with magic is often a slow release. So many people want the 'Hey presto kazzam' with bright flashes and the wow of a rabbit being pulled out of a hat to say – "that is magic," only to find out later that it was a trick.

Real magic is no trick, it is deep rooted and it takes time to unfold.

This is where it is important to find someone who can help with the grieving process. Whatever death we are facing it is important to do exactly that and face it. Yet some deaths can be too painful for us to face.

Sometimes people are so close to a tragedy that they are not ready to transform the suffering. I believe having someone who is able to take on that role for the community is an imperative part of the healing process.

It takes a lot to be a vessel for a community's sorrow. I imagine that all indigenous societies have practiced keening in some form. I do not know how many of them have implemented the aspect of the bridge — the joy — that allows death to be fully celebrated so that new life can be born from the newly discovered peace.

It wasn't something that I found written down anywhere in my research into the 'Celtic' indigenous medicine tradition. And yet it was! I love that my 'Celtic' ancestors left clues hidden in the spaces between the spaces. This is where powerful magic resides. This idea to work with the music of the Dagda's Harp came from lifting text off the page to living the song that is singing in the subtext of the story. When I discovered that I could become Uaithne, the Dagda's Harp and Harper I dedicated energy towards learning to play this instrument firstly for myself and now as part of the great symphony of life.

BEING A HARPER

To be a proficient harper one must first master the art. I came to the harp early in life before I had even heard of the name Uaithne. It was not the death of a person or an animal that awakened me to the medicine inherent in the strings of the harp, it was a series of deaths that led to a primal scream being unleashed from my bodies creating space for joy and ultimately peace.

It was 1974 and I was 11 years old. I had moved from a small junior school to a much larger middle school. I was originally assigned to a classroom that was a year below my level. I tried to explain to the teacher that I was in the wrong grade and at first she did not believe me. When I eventually moved to my correct classroom, all of the kids had already settled in. I felt on the outside from the beginning.

This new school was overwhelming for me. My two favourite things in life at that age were playing football and acting. I was very small for my age and where I had been given opportunities to play football in the junior school I never got a kick in the new one. I remember one day when the teacher took a class of 25 boys onto the top field and divided us into two teams of eleven so that we could have a game. I am sure your maths has brought you to the conclusion that we had three left over. I was one of the three who was given a ball to go and have a kick about with the other two lads that weren't chosen while the rest got stuck into a game.

I was over the moon when I found out that we had drama at middle school. My joy was short-lived. The theatre teacher overlooked me for any involvement when it came to plays. We both auditioned for the same part with a local amateur dramatic group and she was livid that I got the part! After that, I was well and truly left in the wings.

With no football and no theatre in school I then faced another death — that of friendship. My best friend from infant and junior school who lived close by to me, who I walked to school with, sat next to in our shared classes and ate my lunch with, decided he wanted to sit and hang out with the 'cool' kids. I was dropped like a hot potato. I was also living a lie. I had taken up ballet at the local 'Tinkler School of Dance.' I received mixed messages about letting people know I was dancing because it was thought I would get teased by my peers. The daft thing was that quite a few of the girls in school danced with me so it wasn't exactly a secret. The great news was that as a dancer, I got to be in the local pantomime at the theatre. My safe place in all of this was the magic that I felt inside of me when I stepped out under the lights to tread upon the boards.

The pantomime that year was "Babes in the Wood" and I was selected to have a main part as one of the "babes." It is rare for children to take a leading role during this annual UK Christmas show which has its roots in Commedia dell'arte. I had many lines and an abundance of scenes. In those days the panto season ran from mid December all the way until mid February. There were three sets of babes and we took it in turns to perform. Every third show I stepped into the nervous energy, the array of colours, the costumes, the lights and the magic of this interactive theatre experience. With so many matinees as well as evening performances, I was a fixture behind the scenes and on the stage. There was a large cast of professional actors and dancers and as one of the main characters I got to know the adults in the company quite well. I came to see them as my extended family. It was a rarity for boys to be in the 'Tinkler School of Dance,' I was fully aware of that for I was the only one! Being the only boy in the whole cast I received a lot of positive attention. I was on a fabulous high, all of the other deaths that I had experienced in my new school were pushed aside as I rode the wave of euphoria — and then it ended. The panto packed up and left town. As the realisation hit home that this magical doorway had closed and I would never see this group of people again, my world collapsed. I remember sitting on my bed and howling.

As I reflect on that experience through my adult eyes I believe that I wailed not only on my raw grief from the death of the pantomime. The other deaths trapped in my bodies came flooding through — my tears were uncontrollable.

Somewhere inside of me I knew I had to thrash my body around and let it all out. This is what I did and I am thankful I was given the space to do it. I remember my Mum sitting on my bed holding space for me to weep. She was there for me throughout the process without ever looking to suffocate my pain. Once I had released all of the sorrow I then naturally activated the magic of the harp — I plucked the strand of joy.

My Mum bought me a scrapbook. I collected my photos of the cast and pasted them alongside all of the photos of other plays that I had taken part in. The memories captured on film, though in black and white, connected me to the colourful magic of those moments. I found myself transported to a remembrance of smells, sounds, the overwhelming feeling of joy that was in my bodies from my experiences. This led me to finding the strand of peace. To this day I love flicking through those old photos and of course going to the pantomime. I have taken part, written and produced a few in my lifetime and I revel in the idea that I will do so again!

BEING THE HARP

In July 2009 the magical gift of the Dagda's Harp took a twist to sink more deeply into my bones. Spirit took me through an initiation to show me how profound it is to cleanse our bodies through this Medicine Way.

I was going through a long drawn out breakup of a relationship and the woman who I had been living with was on the verge of moving out. There were piles of boxes stuffed full of her belongings stacked high in the living room. I was due to fly to Scotland to lead a pilgrimage and the night before leaving I had a vivid dream. I awoke with a clear remembrance of it. I dreamt that I was at the airport and when I presented my passport at the check-in desk it had fallen open to show the face of my son. I was unable to board as I had picked up his passport instead of my own. With the memory of this scene firmly fixed in my head, I jumped out of bed grabbed my carry-on bag and riffled through it to find my passport. You can imagine the look of incredulity on my face when I flipped it open to see my son's face staring back at me.

I raced through to my office, pulled open the desk drawer where I kept my passport and was startled to see that it was not there. I panicked, I was no longer in my body, I charged through the house, spinning out. I pulled open drawers spilling contents onto the floor as I desperately searched for the missing documents.

Every now and then I would glare at those packed boxes wondering if my passport had mistakenly been sealed inside one of them. I had less than two hours before I was due to leave. I knew that it would be impossible to expedite a new passport before my plane took off. I had a group of ten pilgrims who had paid good money on my promise to meet them at Glasgow airport to lead them on a nine night/ten day pilgrimage to Iona and the Isle of Mull. I had the cushion of one day in Scotland to rest up and shake off the jet lag before collecting them the following day. I was fully aware that I would not be able to process documents within twenty-four hours even if I could change my flight. Clinging to the outside chance that this was possible brought me to the realisation of an overnight with little to no sleep. Arriving to drive a minibus packed with pilgrims in this state was a recipe for disaster. I either found the passport or I was doomed.

As fear gripped tightly across my chest and spread thickly through my slender frame I felt desperation, acute sorrow, frustration, anger, and a huge sense of guilt surging through all three of my bodies. What I offer on pilgrimage is a special service. I drive the vehicle and know the hidden places. The stories and I hold exceptional space for people to meet themselves, make relationship with the land and to grow exponentially from their experience. It wasn't like I could make a call and get someone to step in and take my place.

I kept having flashes of smiling faces turning into concerned anxious and angry faces. I saw the furious features of those pilgrims who had put their trust in me — and thought that I was about to let them down.

I finally ran out of places to look; it felt as if everything was closing in on me. I was tempted to rip open the packed boxes of my ex partner. Instead I stumbled out of the front door and into my garden. I lived in what we call 'noddy land' in the UK and what I refer to as 'cookie cutter world' in the USA. All of the houses looked the same, crammed together with a small patch of lawn front and back. I flung myself onto the grass and I keened. I am sure the neighbours were staring out of their windows. From an outsider's perspective the throes of wild wailing probably looked like someone has lost the plot. I am sure there were people pointing towards the "crazy" person who was writhing around the garden in this suburban neighbourhood!

I let it all out, oblivious to the eyes of curious onlookers. When the sorrow was spent from my bones I breathed in the essence of joy. I flooded my body with my trust in Spirit as the guiding force of my life. Everything happens for a reason — in the height of the illusion of despair a ray of hope shines forth for those who are willing to believe. This was an involuntary keen whereby Spirit flooded through my core filling my pores with heartfelt hope. It was a huge lesson in the full-bodied keen. On hindsight I fully believe had I not surrendered to the three strands plucking the sinews on my bones, I would have kept myself tethered to hopelessness. If I had remained in my head, swirling doubts would have grasped at the barbed hooks of an irredeemable story. Instead I felt the relief of joy and the onset of a deep peace permeating my heart, my bones, my body.

After lying with my face pressed into the earth breathing in her scent and feeling waves of peace flowing through me I gently picked myself up. I then walked purposefully back into the house, I moved through the front room, the kitchen and strode through the laundry room opening the door that led to the garage. I went directly to a tall bookcase and bent down, my hand reaching instinctively towards a journal which was full of notes from past pilgrimages in Ireland. I pulled this purple-bound book from the shelf, opened it up to a page with writings on Tara, the seat of the High King and the heart of Sovereignty and stared jubilantly at my passport!

When I think back to that day I get goose pimples. It was an act of pure magic! Spirit carried me to the book. Magic is indeed within us and around us in each and every moment. We do not have to go to far-flung pockets of this earth in search of it, we need only be present in our lives to access it.

Yet I know my travels and my connection to the land has opened the gateway of presence inside of me. Stepping away from our everyday lives and entering a passageway to pilgrimage offers us a chance of multiple deaths and rebirths. I have learnt from years of dancing in the veil of these profound journeys that we are both witness and the author of our own delicious story. In the presence of ourselves and the natural world we access a portal to understanding — that we are both the doorway and the key to opening up our greatest gifts — the treasures that dwell within.

The words of Oliver Wendell Holmes "Most people die with their music still in them" has always struck a chord with me. I believe it is time to turn this saying on its head and allow our music fully out to play in our lifetime. To do so we need to activate our own inner harp and have the courage and foresight to be Uaithne.

A crow dances with the intimacy of death; a raven strips everything clean. Their sharp beaks peck into the tiniest crevices until all that is left is the bare bones. I believe it is time to channel our inner crow and raven. When we no longer deny death, it can be embraced, accepted and ultimately celebrated.

In the words of Rainer Maria Rilke "Death is our friend precisely because it brings us into absolute and passionate presence with all that is here, that is natural, that is love."

CHAPTER 9: MAGICAL CROWS, RAVENS AND THE CELEBRATION OF DEATH

A PRIVATE AFFAIR

As we have embraced the faster pace of the technological age we have separated ourselves from the natural world and in so doing I believe we have separated ourselves from the true nature of our soul. From my experience I have witnessed the masses shutting the gateway to their feelings. All of this has led to our grief becoming a private affair. The relationship that the Western world has with death has shifted significantly over the span of the last three generations.

FUNERAL

I wonder how many of us have prepared our funeral celebrations? I have requested a wake once I have taken my last breath on the planet. I hope that my children both outlive me yet if they were to go before me, I would sing them home handsomely. I have talked with them both about my wishes and I love that my son announced that he will wear bright pink from head to toe in celebration of my life. I certainly would like a lot of colour and please no black at my 'going home' party.

I believe having conversations about our wishes for our death celebrations is incredibly healthy. My family know that I am to be cremated and that my ashes are to be spread across a glorious road of adventure. I have many favourite places, nemetons, that I have spent time in, both on my own travels and in leading pilgrimages throughout the British Isles and Ireland. I also have earmarked special places dotted around the globe in India, Jamaica, the USA and Canada. I have set the intending that any friend or relative who is up for an adventure can head to one of these magical places to scatter some of my ashes — they include Merlin's Cave at sunrise, Dun I in the betwixt and between of a no moon morning, the Morrighan's Cave on a full moon night, South Cliff, Varkala at the time of the Crow Festival, Skellig Michael on a day that Manannan Mac Lir allows a safe crossing, and

Spoutwood Farm, the home for many years of the Pennsylvania Faerie Festival amongst several others. Setting out on adventure to offer my ashes in these majestic locations will provide the carrier with a story of their own whilst blessing the story of my life.

At my wake I will be laid out in my finest attire — my raven and phoenix cloak, my dented leather top hat and my dragon shoes, one red and one purple, that have the sun and moon decorated upon them. When I am cremated these clothes will be removed and I will have the attendees at my funeral party build a wicker man out of them. A sacred fire will be set outside and people can 'mud up' in my honour. I have a plaster mould cast of my face that will be part of the wicker man offering that'll be burnt as my loved ones sing me home.

I know the three strands of poetry will be plucked with abandon. Stories will be woven on the wind, poetry recited, spirit songs and playful songs to echo through the night and a whole lot of drumming and dancing. I have chosen a list of my favourite songs to be interlaced through the celebrations. It will be a drug and alcohol free bash with a vegetarian feast including plenty of tasty Indian food! I have had such fun putting it together and I am sure those who come to play and pray will have a fabulous time as I dance my way home.

WAKES

In my great grandparents' day wakes were common practice. When someone passed over, my relatives would lay out the body of the deceased in the parlour of their home. For three nights and three days the corpse would lie uncovered in a coffin while friends and family filed in to pay their last respects.

This practice has been part and parcel of my family's story. My Grandad on my father's side was in his 70's when he attended his sister in law Lily's funeral. The old traditions were still strong and Lily's body was laid on the parlour table for viewing. During the pre-funeral party, a stream of guests came to pay their respects and celebrate Lily. As my Grandad stood by the coffin paying his respects he doubled over in pain and slumped to the floor and died from a heart attack. He was then laid to rest on the floor as the celebrations continued. When Lily's body was lifted off the table and taken to the cemetery, his body was lifted up and laid to rest upon the table and a second wake was held!

This ritual of letting a body lie is as important for the being who is going through the acceptance and transition of their own death as it is for those who are left behind to mourn and ultimately celebrate the death.

I wonder if the three nights and days within my family's tradition of the wake has its roots connected to the 'Celtic' medicine of the Dagda's Harp?

STUCK IN STORIES

Leaving a body to lie for three nights and three days gives an opportunity for the being who is in the transition of death time to come to terms with it. Over the course of the wake they have time to adjust to this new experience of no longer having a physical body. It is a certainly a gentle way for them to begin their dance home across the rainbow bridge. It also gifts those left behind three nights and three days to release their sorrow, greet their joy and meet and make their peace.

My understanding of the death process is that we exit the body through what the 'Celtic' people believe is the seat of the soul and vessel of wisdom — the head. I have instructed my loved ones to tap me on the top of my head when I die to let me know that the physical body has passed, especially if my body has to be moved!

Hand in hand with the fear of death in the Western world is our desire to possess and own so much stuff.

Leading pilgrimages over the years has taught me that people overpack. I send out a list of suggested packing items and stress 'pack lightly' and time and time again people turn up with bags twice as large as recommended. Take a look around your own house. If you have an attic and/or a basement, how much stuff is hoarded there? How many people have a garage that they cannot fit their car into because they have piles of stuff blocking the way? I warrant that a lot of people will have boxes in storage that have not seen the light of day for several years. In fact some of these boxes will be a mystery to them, where they have no clue to what is actually inside.

Add to this the fact of our obsession with possessing the land. So much of the earth is being parcelled up for profit. Albeit for business purposes or for the constant demand for housing, trees and habitats are constantly being uprooted across the world. It seems humans have an insatiable appetite to raid the Earth's core of its treasures for a variety of reasons including fossil fuels, crystal collections and/or exotic jewellery.

We even extend the yearning for possession to other people — many seeking a partner, their soul mate to walk by their side. Then they co-create a relationship that looks to possess the other person rather than offering sovereignty to them.

We have so many cords that get attached to people and the aptly named word of our *possessions*. In this way one's energy becomes tightly wrapped, creating knots in our relationships. Is it any wonder people become tethered to their loved ones, to the land and to their vast accumulation of stuff!

There are situations where a loved one is ready to go home. They know it is their time however family members and friends profess a need for them to still be there for them. They claw and fight to keep the person alive. They wrap them in so many cords that when the person passes the cords often snag, keeping them trapped to an earthly body that no longer has any life force within it.

With all of this possession going on is it any wonder that when a person's heart stops beating, they do not always go home. Add to this the unexpected deaths, the challenging way some people meet death, the mass displacement that has taken place in the story of the world — and it becomes clear to see why we have a huge amount of trapped energy. My work has taught me that there are so many lost and displaced souls that float around in the ethers.

It is why each year we gather to honour the backbone of a 'Celtic' Medicine Way and weave the Wild Hunt — to sing home the souls of the dead. It is why the Hindus gather each year to celebrate the Crow Festival in Varkala.

THE LAND MIRRORS THE WORK

After sweeping our bodies clean, plucking the 3 strands on the South Cliff beach, we stood and watched the song of the land mirror our work. The clouds swept in on the wind, bulbous, silver-sheened and grey, the light shifted dramatically and the heavens opened in a cleansing downpour. We all sauntered up the winding staircase to the retreat centre, enjoying the refreshing monsoon rain soaking our clothes and cooling our skin. Each of us seemed to walk taller and I am sure we all felt so much lighter and brighter.

Pat and I were to witness another piece of crow magic before the rains had been released, the wind had ceased and clear blue skies brought a deep sense of joy and a full measure of peace to the land.

THE SECOND COMING

Pat and I made a cup of tea and sat outside our room on the balcony. Within seconds a crow, which I believe was the same crow that had visited us before, landed on the exact same branch and looked intently at us. The wind whipped the branches of the tree yet the crow held its own. As the tree swayed, so the crow went into a ritual that had us both sitting on the edge of our seats in amazement.

Just as the land was mirroring our work, the crow joined the song of the harp. Its voice shrieked onto the wind and then it preened itself. For several minutes the crow pecked and cleansed each part of its body — lifting its wings one at a time and running its beak across all of its body until the rains stopped and the wind stilled. The crow then looked into our awestruck eyes and it sat peacefully upon the branch for several heartbeats before powerfully flying off towards the shining sun.

BIRDS OF THE NORTH

In the 'Celtic' tradition I work with the Crow and Raven in the North and also the king of the birds, the Eagle. This gateway is all about speaking our truth, being in integrity and authenticity. The South is about standing in the power of our song, music, dance, poetry, living our stories and bringing our joy, love and laughter to the world. On the South Cliff we stirred the Northern Gateway medicine honouring the ancestors and all life.

The morning of the Festival I sat on the balcony and watched an eagle fly in from the West. The Western Gateway in my tradition connects to vison, hope, creativity and illumination. As I pondered on the second coming of the crow, I was blessed by this eagle who flew under the overhang of our balcony roof gently skimming the wall as it circled inches over my head then flew out, returning to the West from where it had begun.

My heart thumped and I breathed deeply as I processed the sheer power of the eagle's blessing upon me. Nature is always sharing its story and I thought of Branwen and Rhiannon who both had found ways to communicate with birds and they with them.

I thought about my own life and the message of the eagle. My lesson here is a simple one — if I am willing to be an authentic vessel of integrity on the planet, with the courage to bring the truth of my voice to the world, then I will have the freedom to fly into my visions, bringing my joy, my dance, the poetry of my life as the High King/High Queen of my own life story made manifest.

If, on the other hand, I let ego rule my heart and I hide from my self and others in inauthentic ways, I will not graze the wall gently, I will smash into it. The inauthentic pathway hiding behind fake masks leads to self-imposed walls built on the decay of a festering wounded wasteland.

As clear as I have become walking and working a Medicine Way I felt the shifts of everything going deeper.

I wonder how many of us are willing to let the fullness of our creativity out to play? To release the constraints of what other people think of us so that we fly with true freedom in the world. Who is willing to add their light with a purity and an integrity to help all beings prosper? More importantly, am I? Each of us is the architect, author and either the authentic hero or inauthentic fool.

THE FESTIVAL OF THE CROW

On the morning of the festival, we followed the same pathway that I had taken four years previously to Papansam beach. We joined the throng of merrymakers heading to honour all life. We went as witnesses to the celebrations of the thousands gathered there on no moon day.

It was the hottest day since our arrival in India which made — perfect sense to me. For on this the day of the darkest moon we were met by the brightest sun!

On our arrival back at the retreat centre, Anuraj had kindly prepared a tray of offerings along with five banana leaves and a large bowl of fruit for the crows to feast upon.

We once again took the winding staircase, carrying the offerings, down to an empty beach on the South Cliff side. With a fire lit on the beach and speaking to the flames, we sang a song that sings us, Amrun, and we took turns cleansing in the raw power of the ocean.

There was a strong undertow so we were deeply rooted to support each other. We dipped our bodies three times into the surging tide. The force of the water took my breath away. I remember crawling before standing after submerging my body for the third time. A trail of sand oozed out of my belly button looking like an umbilical cord.

We all then joined in a circle to give thanks and as we gave gratitude to the ancestors, the biggest wave of the day swept across the beach reaching all of the way to the steps leading back up to the retreat centre. We burst into joyous laughter feeling the voice of Spirit thanking us as we thanked all beings.

Five Indian youths who had stood off to the side watching us now approached and one held both his hands in the air showing five digits on each hand. I took this as meaning Sovereignty in both the sacred feminine and masculine. He then reached out his right hand, the masculine and touched his index finger to my heart. His finger connected with the crow tattoo upon my chest that has five aspects of the goddess within the design.

He had the broadest smile and as I later processed that interaction I reflected on the importance for each of us to take responsibility for healing the sacred masculine and feminine within our own hearts.

We returned to our balcony and I felt sure that the crow would come soon for the third time.

BORN FROM THE SEA

The crow did not come that day. Instead I received a video message from my daughter in the UK. It was a piece of icing on the cake — my beautiful grandaughter Muirín crawled for the first time that day. As we had crawled from the sea, born anew during the Festival of the Crow, she had crawled. Her name means — "Born from the Sea!"

FEROZ AND THE CROW

Feroz visited the retreat centre again and was keen to know if the crows had come to visit. I shared the experience Pat and I had had with our two visits. As I explained how the crow had sung with its neck stretched out and its wings back he looked at me and said in earnest "Crow was like a peacock."

I love how Spirit works. He had no idea that I had shared the Crow and Peacock story and yet there he was bringing strands of the magic together.

Spirit brought more strands together the next day. From my balcony I saw a bird that I had never laid eyes on before. It had a black body and looked distinctly like a crow except that it had rich golden brown wings and a long tail just like a peacock. It even walked like a peacock! I went down to have breakfast and asked Anuraj what kind of bird it was. As I sat at the breakfast table waiting for Anuraj to appear an actual peacock strutted by. If you could have seen my face!

My thoughts were — how applicable is that —
transformation was happening. It felt like the crow and
the peacock were both flying free while at the same
time merging with each other.

Anuraj shared that the bird I had seen is a Greater
Coucal which he considers as part of the crow family.
It is otherwise known as a Crow Pheasant!

THE SONG OF THE BOATMAN

To honour the backwaters of Kerala we hired a green
boat, a boat that is propelled through the water without
the use of an engine. The majestic backwaters in
Kerala have been severely affected by the tourist
industry. I wrote about the desecration of these waters
in "13 Steps to Bringing Magic into Your Life." We
had initially wanted to go on an overnight excursion on
a different stretch of water. However, there were no
green boats available to us. We therefore chose a day
trip and headed to weave Amrun in support of the
transformation of these treasured waters. Along with
our heartsong, we added a blessing that we had

brought with us from holy springs, wells, rivers and lakes from Scotland, Ireland, England, Canada and the USA. Waters that had been prayed on during ceremonies were prayed on again. Our guide Ramanan who expertly steered us through the maze of waterways joined his baritone voice to our song and the five of us aboard brought the magic of our light to this gentle nemeton of southern India.

I looked up the name Ramanan on our return to the retreat centre and I revelled in discovering that it means "delighting."

AMBU CALLS THROUGH THE ETHERS

Another thread came on the journey home to the Ayurvedic centre. We stopped behind a bus that had the name Ambu emblazoned on it, which, if you remember from earlier, is the name of the man who shared the story of the Crow Festival. And his name means "water!" We had literally just worked a beautiful water ritual the day after weaving deeply with the Crow Festival. It felt so appropriate to feel his touch through the ethers.

A THIRD VISIT

I knew the crow would return for a third visit. It is the 'Celtic' way! Pat and I were blessed with its company that night as we packed our bags in preparation to leave the following morning. Pat had left a bag of dates out on the balcony and while we were away the crows came in and helped themselves to the tasty treat. She had picked up the bag leaving four dates lying on the balcony floor. They were lying in the corner of the balcony furthest away from the doorway into our bedroom. We had retreated into our sitting room/dressing room where our suitcases and clothes were stored in a large wardrobe.

As we rolled our clothes into our suitcases there was a loud burst of crow song. It was such a vociferous cry that I stood up and walked into the bedroom to see what the crow was wanting to say to us. I fully expected it to be on the balcony by the dates. Instead I stepped into the bedroom right in front of the crow. It was in the middle of the room on the floor looking directly at me and singing for all it was worth. The crow had flown through the open balcony doorway and was hopping contentedly around the bedroom! My jaw must have been close to grazing the ground!

It looked intently towards me as it sat by the foot of the bed singing freely and without a care in the world. It then took to wing and flew to perch on the chair outside that I sat on each day. It looked towards Pat and me and continued singing. I slowly followed it out whereby it hopped onto the balcony railing. With what appeared to be a twinkle in its eye and a joyous burst of song, it flew down and picked up a date and then flew on its way.

A murder of crows then appeared and the song of gratitude swept through the air. I will treasure the three individual crow visits and how the collective crows came in at the beginning of this journey four years previously and at the end of this one in 2017. The magic of these interactions will live in my heart forever and a day!

As for the three dates left behind — were they significant? Magic is everywhere, within us and around us. When we gather with a strong intending to work alongside spirit I find the magic intensifies. The healing properties of dates are many including helping ease the birthing process. Alongside this is the fact that three dates were left behind. I took from this message that those of us gathered to celebrate the Crow Festival all have a date with the birthing of significant new pieces in our physical, mental and spiritual bodies.

THE BIRTHING OF THIS BOOK

It was on the dark moon, no moon day of February 2018 that I journeyed to Spirit to ask for guidance as to what I was to write next. I had so many ideas flowing in it became quite overwhelming. I knew I needed help in focusing. Spirit was clear. I was shown a number of books honouring magical encounters that I have had in my life and I was asked to start by sharing a book that honoured the Crow Nation followed by one that celebrated my interactions with elephants. When I came out of the journey my partner Joyce said "Look outside at that cloud — it looks like a crow perched on an elephant's back." I then shared my journey and her reply was "You can't write this shit."

THE CROW MOON MEETS THE BEAST FROM THE EAST

On the first full moon of March 2018 I was beamed live to 55 different countries through Sounds True's Year of Ceremony. When I had been invited to lead a full moon ceremony I had chosen one of the two dates that were available and the March date was the best one for my calendar. I learned as I prepared for the online gathering that one of the names of the March full moon is the "Crow Moon."

The Morrighan was well and truly with us that night. Unlike some of their broadcasts I had the great fortune of leading the ceremony directly into the zenith of the full moon. The time of each full moon varies each · month and this one reached its zenith on Friday March

2nd at 12.51am Scottish time. I went live at midnight through to 1.30am!

Thursday 1st March brought the "Beast from the East." This was the name given to a mighty snowstorm that resulted from an Arctic breakout transporting cold air from Siberia and bringing heaps of snow throughout the British Isles. I live in a small coastal village in the Kingdom of Fife, Scotland. We rarely see any accumulation here yet on that Thursday we were snowed in. Watching the waves pounding against the shoreline was dramatic as the snow fell all around us. At 10pm that night Joyce and I walked down to the beach. There was snow covering the sand as the storm continued to rage. We walked in the betwixt and between of the outgoing tide and sang to thank Spirit for the support for the upcoming ceremony. The sky was heavy with snow and as we sang, for a brief moment in time, the clouds parted to reveal the full moon shining down upon us. We felt incredibly blessed. We then returned home and put on my CD of Spirit Songs "Sacred Outcast." Dancing and singing

the Morrighan song just before going live felt
incredibly empowering.

We knew she was with us, as were many guides that
night, for the storm was the most testing weather we
have experienced for many years here in the UK. We
were on a red warning. So many roads were closed,
traffic was stuck, hospital operations cancelled,
schools closed, rail and air service disrupted and many
homes were without power.

We were blessed to have an internet connection to lead
the ceremony!

JAMES COSMO

I had seen a Scottish man who is an actor at the
Glasgow airport around Samhain, October 2017. I was
on my way home from the USA via Heathrow airport
to Glasgow. I had been overseas leading the Wild Hunt
for the nineteenth time. This rich work is supported big
time by the Morrighan. She has gifted me with
particular rituals to help participants cleanse and

prepare for the intensity of this ceremony.

The actor in question had travelled to Scotland from Heathrow on the same plane as I had. I am not great with remembering names and yet I knew his face. I explained what he looked like and Joyce identified him as James Cosmo.

He then appeared on a TV advertisement during the cycle of the Crow Moon. He popped up onto the screen dressed as a crow. James was the leader of the "Nights Watch" in "Game of Thrones." In the advert he wears his "crow" cloak and says "Don't put off until tomorrow something… something… something" and then a crow is heard singing on the wind.

I felt the call of the crow encouraging me to write, to focus on the stories I wanted to share. It was a quirky amusing way to remind me not to put off the writing until tomorrow, to bring forth the medicine of my words today!

With all of these signs I felt the importance of "Magical Crows, Ravens and the Celebration of Death" being brought to manifestation in the world. So it was started on no moon day in February, weaved through the Crow Moon of March and finished as we moved out of the dark half of the year into the light half of the year at Beltane.

THREE DIFFERENT NOVELS SHARE A MESSAGE

During the weaving of these words I read three books which all had magical messages on the first page for me.

The first was from a book that my partner Joyce had bought for me in December 2016. I had not picked it up to start reading until March a year and a bit later. It is called "Dreamdark — Blackbringer" by Laini Taylor. The first page of Chapter One introduces the reader to the heroine of the story who is a Fae Woman by the name of Magpie Windwitch. I was delighted to discover that she travels around with a protective band of crows who are central to the story. And what a wonderful set of characters they are!

The second book I began at the end of March. The day before I began to read it I had been writing the chapter on the three strands of poetry. I had literally just written about my friends Dr. Michael and Jennifer Fenster's first keening experience when I received a Facebook message from Mike. He sent me a photo of a crow's foot that he found by a pine tree at the hotel he was staying in. He shared how each day he would go down to make offerings honouring the Morrighan and connect with the many crows that were constantly flying around his window. He discovered the foot lying there, no feathers, no other bones, just one long crow's foot.

The next day I began a book called "Dunstan" by Conn Iggulden, set in tenth-century England. The second line reads "Like a crow's foot dipped in ink and dragged across the page, my hands shake so. Shall I sand these black scratchings from this fine vellum?"

My heart swelled with gratitude and I felt inspired by the messages that were constantly coming through the ethers.

I was then writing the chapter on the 3 strands when I began reading a third book "Let Me Lie" by Clare Mackintosh in late April. She offered these words on the first page "Death does not suit me. I wear it like a borrowed coat; it slips off my shoulders and trails in the dirt. It is ill-fitting, uncomfortable. I want to shrug it off, to throw it in the cupboard and take back my well-tailored clothes. I didn't want to leave my old life, but I am hopeful for my next one – hopeful I can become someone beautiful and vibrant. For now, I am trapped. Between lives. In limbo."

As I digested these words I felt a tickle go down my spine as I had been reviewing the chapter on the Crow Festival and the importance of helping souls who have been trapped without bodies to go home.

My experience is that the Universe is always talking to us and when we listen – magic happens. The magic heightened during the creative writing of these nine chapters!

MAGICAL CONNECTIONS INTENSIFY

The connection to crows and ravens and the celebration of death intensified as I wrote.

I received a wonderful picture of an amazing pair of boots made by Catskill Moccasins. A majestic purple raven was embellished on each boot. The photo came with a message that was sent by people who rarely get in touch with me saying "These look like your boots."

My massage therapist shared that she has a pair of ravens nesting in the field behind her house. She lives at 5 Raven Crescent with a postcode of ER1. Royal ravens indeed!

THE MORRIGHAN AND A QUEST FOR THE HOLY GRAIL

One of my students, who recently completed her study of a 3-Year 'Celtic' shamanic pathway with me, travelled on my pilgrimage to Cornwall in May 2018. The Beltane moon was in Scorpio on Monday April 30th. It was intensely beautiful and offered wonderful opportunities for release. I worked with a new two-year group leading into the full moon and then I headed to Cornwall to lead the pilgrimage.

I shared the story of Parzival and the Holy Grail on the craggy rocks where the river Trevillet flows into the Celtic sea. We then took the trail through the faerie woods strewn with bluebells and all bathed individually at the goddess stone in the waters of St. Nectan's. This spot is where legend has the Knights of the Round Table bathing before going on their quest to seek the grail. We made oaths at the waterfall. I made mine to find, honour and share the gifts of my inner grail. I spoke to the Morrighan to support the deepening of my relationship with Sovereignty. As I plunged my body into the sparkling waters I felt the call to be the roots, heart and wings of integrity, to shine even more authentically and speak my truth with increased courage in the world.

The following day I climbed up on the cliffs opposite Merlin's Cave and keened. My own quest for the inner grail asks me to bring the heart of the Fisher-King through the courage of Parzival. This way I will create a thriving kingdom. If I play small in the world and come from my head, from my ego and from fear, I will be as Amfortas, a Fisher-King that festers in a wounded wasteland.

Natalya, whose name means "birth" joined me to drum and hold space while I keened. I then drummed and held space for her to keen. What I love is how I had left Scotland without my drum. I was not sure there would be space for it in the vehicle so I left it in the Kingdom of Fife. Before driving south to Cornwall I stopped in Glasgow where Joyce has a drum. I shared I had regretted not bringing the drum and she had said I could take her drum "however it may not want to come." When I say "my drum" and "her drum," — we are the guardians of these drums, not the owners. If you work with a drum you will know that they have personalities of their own. The drums carry us — they are medicine pieces!

Both Joyce and I knew that "her drum" was staying firmly put. Knowing that Natalya was driving down to Cornwall in her car it prompted me to ask her to bring a drum. A magical story was in the brewing! This third drum was also a new drum, gifted to Natalya for a recent birthday.

I love how Spirit works. The number 3 is important in the 'Celtic' world for many reasons – life-death-rebirth, the daylight - nighttime -and the betwixt and between, mother - maiden - crone, the three aspects of the Morrighan, the Dagda's three daughters all named Brighid, the three Strands of Poetry and the list goes on…

Whenever I ask my students to undertake a huge medicine piece I will do the same. I recently invited my two-year group to begin a 13-moon journey beginning on the Beltane moon 2018. This entails meeting with a full moon partner each month over the next 13 moons. This cycle begins with the birthing time of the light half of the year, Beltane, continues into the dark half of the year, Samhain, and culminates with our last gathering of the two-year program in the Kingdom of Fife on the Beltane moon of 2019.

As my students engage in this 13-moon experience I do too. My full moon partner is Natalya. Each month we submit our visions, a list of what we desire to accomplish for the following moon. Then when that full moon comes around, we submit a new list for the next month, while talking through our progress for the moon we have just lived under.

We offer gentle strength in holding each other and ourselves accountable for stirring the cauldron of our visions.

So as I stood on the rugged Cornish cliffs I was invited to work with the new drum that carries Natalya. I had asked Natalya to check in with the drum the previous evening to make sure that I had permission to handle it. In our Western society we are quick to grab things and scatter our DNA all over the place. In a Medicine Way one never touches another person's jewellery, drum, rattle or indeed any medicine tools without permission. For those who are unfamiliar with this practice — the medicine person then asks the drum, or whatever tool is to be passed into another person's hands, whether it is okay for that to happen. As I have said, we are guardians of these tools rather than the owners!

I would have been surprised if this drum had said no because it was made in honour of the Morrighan. Having spent years working closely with the Morrighan I have a constant connection to her.

The drum came to Natalya through a magical story. It was gifted to her for her 40th birthday. The woman who birthed, (created) the drum is Suzy Crockford of Dartmoor drums in the UK. Suzy works with the land in an ethical way resourcing materials locally and with the greatest respect. She journeyed to the Spirit world for guidance on what drum she was to make for Natalya and was surprised to find that the drum had already been made. Suzy had birthed a drum for herself, however she had never consecrated it as her guidance told her that it was not the drum for her. It was this drum, the Morrighan's Drum.

When Natalya contacted Suzy, Suzy was shown that Natalya's deep work with the Morrighan meant that the drum was meant for her.

Just before Natalya talked with Suzy she received my invitation to be my full moon partner for the thirteen moons. Interestingly the drum has thirteen sides. The painting on the drum is of a crow emerging in flight from a chalice that has the deep roots of a tree!

Suzy's husband painted the design upon the drum which was then passed to two friends of Natalya's who gifted the drum to her for her 40th birthday.

Numbers and names have always fascinated me. Natalya was the third person to handle the drum. It was passed through the birthing process of the masculine and feminine, first Suzy and her husband Fergus. The name Suzy means "Lily" — Lily means "innocence, purity, peace and unconditional love." Fergus means "strong virile warrior." A phenomenal combination of gifts to carry this medicine into the world!

The drum was then sent to Natalya's friends Elisa and Christoph whose names mean "God is my oath," and "He who holds Christ in his heart." They handed the packaged drum to Natalya — a sacred gift from the feminine and masculine.

Natalya was then the third person to hold the drum. Her friends who have no knowledge of shamanism, sweetly and intuitively waited for permission from Natalya before they also handled the drum.

At St. Nectan's Waterfall I had asked the pilgrims in which order they would like to go to meet, bathe and make oaths in the pool of water. There were six of us and I made all six spots available. My placement was to be allocated by Spirit. I waited for all five pilgrims to choose and the last space was not chosen so it became mine. I was sixth in line.

Adding an extra depth of spice to the proceedings — there were three women and three men who bathed that day. A woman named Bridget followed by a man named Carl, a woman Kyra, a man Jon, Natalya, and then myself.

As Natalya and I sang Amrun into the ethers we peeled off one by one, bathed and then dressed before the next person met the waters. I see the significance now of the seventh pilgrim Pam choosing to stay behind and rest that day. We represented the balance of the feminine and masculine in all three bodies, the physical, mental and spiritual. We were cleansing our own bodies in preparation for seeking our own inner grail while holding space for major shifts in the collective!

As for the collective name of our party — we were the "exalted one, with freedom, an enthroned goddess, a gift of god, a birth-day and a strong courageous manly one"!

I was both the six person to bathe and the sixth person to handle the Morrighan drum which had passed through Suzy, Fergus, Elisa, Christoph, Natalya to me.

Again three women and three men. The feminine-masculine balance of the three worlds (upper, middle and lower) and the healing of the three bodies (physical, mental and spiritual) were represented here. I feel that the significance of the three women and men both with the drum and at the waterfall are part of a much deeper richer story. There is always so much magic in the folds of our lives!

One other number that was part of the equation is Thirteen. It is the number of transformation. The obvious connection here is to the 13 moon journey and the thirteen sides of the Morrighan drum. Yet there is also a third aspect. Natalya celebrated her 40th birthday to receive this gift and I am 54 years young. $4 + 0 + 5 + 4 = 13$. As I say magic is hidden in the folds!

To support our quest for the inner grail each pilgrim had pulled a card from the Wildwood tarot deck that has been beautifully put together by Mark Ryan, John Matthews and Will Worthington. I always have people take a card, look at it and then place it back in the deck in case another person requires the same card. I then invite people to stir the medicine of the card into their own cauldrons before sharing it with others. I have marvelled over the years at how often people draw the same cards. I advocate drawing cards only occasionally as this way the magic does not dissipate.

It is important to remember that we always get what we need, not necessarily what we want. Understanding the significance of the card can open doorways for us in our quest.

Interestingly both Natalya and I found out later that we had both drawn the same card. None other than the Kingfisher. Both of us had the same reaction as we saw the relevance of this journey to the Fisher-King.

I also marvelled at the fact that kingfishers are unlike many other species of birds. The male and female are both brightly coloured! They carry the colours of the rainbow, which connected me to the balance of fire and water and of the divine masculine and feminine within my own three bodies.

As I started to drum for Natalya's keening song, three members of the crow family flew by. The Morrighan taking to wing in that moment was auspicious for a heartbeat later three figures appeared on this secluded stretch of headland. We had tucked ourselves off the main pathway on purpose for privacy as we keened. As the drumbeats met the mist hanging in the air around us, two grown men and one adolescent, a boy on the cusp of manhood, strode by, all carrying fishing rods. The youth stood watching and I could hear Parzival's voice asking "What ails thee?" How amazing was that, a Fisher-King for each of the bodies!

The threads of crow magic, Morrighan magic and the celebration of death for new life sings loud and clear in my heart.

THE RETURN OF RAVENS

Joyce and I found a pair of ravens nesting in our village in March. What a joy it is to see these majestic winged ones living in our own village once more. About a five-minute walk along a lane parallel to the beach they have made their nest high in the boughs of a maple tree. It was so heart-warming to see ravens in our neighbourhood. Our joy increased as we have been seeing them each day in our own garden. They come to bathe in the birdbath and feast on the high quality bird food that we put out each day. I adore magic. As I wrote these words sitting on the patio in my garden, one of the ravens flew right over my head and sang! Such a beautiful confirmation from Spirit.

THE ART OF CELEBRATING DEATH

So many tangible threads supporting the writing. Even the wonderful cover of this book has a deeper story.

Just as Dr. Mike was tuned in because of his involvement writing the foreword for the book — I shared earlier his crow's foot story — so the artist Nicole Pisaniello, whose fabulous artwork adorns the front cover, also had a major Crow experience.

I had been reviewing the Chapter on the Morrighan's Cave which is also known as the Cave of the Cats and I had been delving into the chapter on the importance of plucking the three strands. I then took a break and went on Facebook to check if there were any messages. As Spirit would have it the page loaded with a post of Nicole's looking right at me. She wrote how she and her partner Travis had selflessly reached out to help an abandoned cat. The cat had been horrendously abused. They had nursed it, taken it to the vet and had high hopes for its recovery.

Nicole is extremely connected to crows and ravens. It is why I asked her if she would consider having her artwork on the cover. On the day the cat arrived a crow landed on her roof and sang. Every day afterwards the crow sang long and strong perched on her rooftop. Nicole felt that the little cat in their care was protected. She named him Whispy; he started to respond positively and she felt hopeful.

Then the crow disappeared and Whispy regressed and was humanely euthanized on March 26th 2018 around 4pm.

Nicole's world crumbled. She wrote these words and posted them on Facebook:

"It is a sad reality that we have to learn to deal with and accept death. I've seen lots of animals die and even seen people die, but this situation was particularly cruel and heartbreaking. He had been in great pain. I want to say his name and show a picture of him here so that he doesn't disappear. So that people know that this can be avoided if we only cared more. I didn't give him a name because I thought I was going to keep him or thought he was going to survive (though I did hope). I'm not that naive. He was in the worst shape I have ever seen. I gave it to him because I felt like he deserved to die with a name given to him by a person who loved him and cared about him. We don't know how old he was or how long he'd been out in the woods in the cold. And even though it killed a part of my soul to see this poor creature, who, when he was able to show us parts of his personality, was so very sweet, and even though he didn't make it, I would do it again for the next animal. Because I believe kindness matters. I believe it was better that he had a few nights in a warm bed and died with people who loved him around him than dying out alone in the woods. I will try and help one animal at a time when I'm able. That is worth any hurt that I feel."

"I would do it again, but right now I am not okay. I'm not okay having seen an animal in that kind of condition and knowing how horrible humans are that they could allow this to happen and everything seems ridiculously futile. I'm just really not okay. And I miss him."

As I read Nicole's heartfelt words I knew that I could help her. As she and Travis had helped to provide a safe space for Whispy to prepare for and ultimately meet death, so I could help Nicole fully celebrate his death.

Nicole was hurt and incredibly angry. She was also confused as to why the crow had flown from her rooftop. She felt the crow had abandoned her and without its support Whispy had been called home to the Spirit world.

My first response was that because she had agreed to illustrate the front cover of the book she was intrinsically connected to the writing. I told her how Dr. Mike Fenster had found a crow's foot and shared a photo and information with me on the exact same day I wrote his name in the book and then the following day I had started a new book that spoke of a crow's foot.

I shared that because he was writing the foreword he was part of a deeper journey. The same applied to her. "Magical Crows, Ravens and the Celebration of Death" was reaching through the ethers in mystical ways.

I explained to Nicole that from my perspective the crow hadn't abandoned her. It came to sing Whispy home. So many people keep animals alive beyond their true lifespan because they cannot bear to part with their loved one. It takes courage to honour an animal's passing and the crow knew it was time for Whispy to travel on.

I am also not a regular Facebook user and I know Spirit guided me to Nicole's post. The crow knew that there was a new piece of magic for Nicole to glean from this experience.

I asked her "had she keened before?" Her answer was she had, however as she explained her process I discovered she had left out key ingredients. She knew to pluck the strand of sorrow only. She was well and truly stuck in the story. After I explained the bridges to Nicole and the importance of transforming sorrow to joy to peace, she was able to fully keen and experience the true celebration of death.

ONE FINAL OFFERING

It is with great joy that Joyce and I watched as two baby ravens, born to proud parents in our village, flew above our heads. The ravens are returning!

Magic happens in us and around us all of the time. The crows and ravens speak to us, as all life speaks to us, if only we have the heart and presence of mind to listen.

Death is a natural part of our cycle on the planet and once we learn to cherish it and celebrate it to the full we give space for new life to come flowing through. Here is to Magic, to all of the members of the Corvine family and to life-death-rebirth, in gratitude, Séa.

ABOUT THE AUTHOR

Andrew Steed has dedicated his life to serving others and making love to the land. He puts his heart and soul into his work which has carried him all around the world. From the outside it may seem glamourous — The reality is he is often away from his family and loved ones for weeks/months at a time as he follows the guidance of Spirit. Those who frequent airports and cross time zones regularly will know that it is a lot of work and for Andrew it is incredibly rewarding. He has helped people of all ages through his dynamic storytelling residencies in schools, motivational seminars in Universities, leadership training in corporate companies, pilgrimages, gatherings and workshops in community settings throughout the UK, Ireland, Canada, USA, Jamaica, Barbados and India.

Andrew has been self employed since 1996. He currently has three other books in print, a CD of Spirit Songs and two storytelling CD's all available through Amazon and/or iTunes.

He recently found his heart home on the planet in the Kingdom of Fife where he enjoys amongst many things, strolls on the beach with his partner Joyce and feeding the countless birds that fly into the garden each day.

Look for other books by Andrew:

"13 Steps to Bringing Magic into Your Life"

"Powering Up Our Life Stories"

"The First Santa"

Also available a CD of Songs:

"Sacred Outcast"

And two Storytelling CD's

"In the Roots of the Story"

"Between the Realms"

www.andrewsteed.com

asteed@andrewsteed.com

ABOUT THE ARTIST

Nicole Pisaniello is an artist and performer living in Richmond, Virginia with her partner, Travis, and their cat, Pyramus (Bean). She studied art at Virginia Commonwealth University and began her illustration business shortly after, much inspired by her yearly visits to the May Day Fairie Festival at Spoutwood Farm in Glen Rock, PA, for which she will be forever grateful.

She has been published in "500 Fairy Motifs" by Myrea Petit, Faerie Magazine, and "How to Draw and Paint Fairyland" by Linda Ravenscroft, along side many other wonderful fantasy artists. Most recently she has produced work for the Poe Museum of Richmond in the form of two solo gallery shows based on the works of Edgar Allan Poe.

Nicole's artwork has always been inspired by the Fae and by myths and legends of old. Whatever form her art takes, be it illustration, costumed character performance, or aerial circus, the heart of it is always stories. She has worked closely with Crow over the years both as a guide and an artistic inspiration, and she was simply delighted when Andrew asked her to contribute to this book.

To see more of Nicole's work please visit:

www.nicolepisaniello.com

Instagram: @nicolepisaniello

Facebook: **"The Art of Nicole Pisaniello"**

CPSIA information can be obtained
at www.ICGtesting.com
Printed in the USA
BVHW08s1427131018
530113BV00020B/767/P